sound the trumpet AGAIN!

MORE messages to empower african american men

Z chron 5:11-14

sound the trumpet AGAIN!

MORE messages to empower african american men

edited by darryl d. sims

Judson Press
Valley Forge, Pennsylvania

sound the trumpet AGAIN!

MORE messages to empower african american men

© 2004 by Judson Press, Valley Forge, PA 19482-0851
All rights reserved.

Unless otherwise indicated, Bible quotations in this volume are from the Holy Bible, King James Version. If another version is indicated in a chapter's opening text, all Scriptures quoted within that chapter are from that version as well.

Scriptures marked NRSV are from the New Revised Standard Version of the Bible, copyright 1989, by the Division of Christian Education of the National Council of Churches of Christ in the U.S.A. Used by permission. All rights reserved.

Scriptures marked NKJV are from the New King James Version. Copyright © 1982 by Thomas Nelson, Inc. All rights reserved. Used by permission.

Library of Congress Cataloging-in-Publication Data

Sound the trumpet again! : more messages to empower African American men / edited by Darryl D. Sims.— 1st ed.
    p. cm.
  ISBN 0-8170-1476-4 (alk. paper)
  1. African American men—Religious life. 2. African American men—Conduct of life. 3. Sermons, American—African American authors. I. Sims, Darryl D.
  BV4468.2.A34S67 2004
  248.8'42'08996073—dc22
                                                    2004022751

Printed in the U.S.A.

12 11 10 09 08 07 06 05 04

10 9 8 7 6 5 4 3 2 1

To the handful of people who have taught me in the past year of my life what unconditional love is all about. Leading the class was and is my friend, sister, and mentor, Rev. Dr. Martha Simmons. Right beside her is my venerable pastor/teacher/dad/uncle/friend/advisor/counselor/coach and personal loan officer Dr. Charles Edward Booth, the pastor in whom I am well pleased and blessed to have the privilege to call anytime and discuss anything.

contents

acknowledgments

i acknowledge my brother and friend pastor D. Darryl Griffin of Oakdale Covenant Church in Chicago. My brother and friend Rev. Romal J. Tune of People for the American Way out of Washington, D.C. My Bridgeport, Connecticut, connection, my dearest and most supportive friend in the ministry, Pastor Tyrone P. Jones IV, his lovely wife and my friend, first lady Rev. Elizabeth Jones. And a preacher affectionately referred to as "Bishop," Pastor Anthony Bennett. These people have searched me out and considered it not robbery to embrace me and teach me the authentic and biblical meaning of friendship.

I acknowledge the many pastors who have taken the time out of their demanding lives to remind me that nothing is over until God says it is. These include my main man Pastor Damon Lynch Jr., Pastor Joshua King, Pastor Richard Wills, Pastor Vincent Smith, Pastor Gary Simpson, Pastor Ralph Canty, Pastor Lance Watson, Pastor Dwight Jones, Pastor Angelo V. Chatman, Pastor Robert Scott, Pastor Byron Whitehead, Pastor William Martin, Pastor Harry White, and my proven friend Pastor DeQuincy "DQ" Hentz, who is doing a fantastic job at the Magnificent Mt. Zion Baptist Church in Woodlawn, Ohio.

Then there are some newly found friends that have blessed me in recent times: Howard E. Fitts Sr., Jamal Kemp, Rev. Derrick Jones, Rev. Linda Gresham, Marlin Jamison, Ron Baker Jr., Shalanda White, Konyia Clark, and my homegirl Mrs. Terri Hannett. I thank God for all of you and I thank all of you guys and gals for your love, support, and positive words of encouragement.

I recognize and thank all those who have assisted me specifically with this project. Dr. Donna Y. Ford deserves a great deal of credit for her tireless effort in working closely by my side throughout the organizing and compiling of all the sermons. In addition, she provided assistance in most of the editing. Words can't adequately express my appreciation to such a jewel of a genuine person and friend. I shall always be in her debt.

I would like to acknowledge a few other people who made some form of sacrifice to help facilitate the completion of this book: my youngest brother Le Anthony "Tony" Brown, Aja Carr of Urban Ministries, Inc., Rev. Ricky Georgetown of Chicago State University, Kathy Hill of Chicago State University, Donna Delowell of Richmond, Va., and my friend and sister Rev. Jacqueline Glass, who did an excellent job with the transcribing of some of the tapes.

And I would be remiss not to thank all of the contributors and their secretaries and staff assistants. Among those who have set themselves apart are Tiffany Tisdale of Jacksonville, Florida, Angela Lynch of Brooklyn, New York, Tina DeVeaux of Baltimore, Maryland, and my ace Mrs. Debra Daniels of West Dallas, Texas. Finally, I must acknowledge the "faithful few": Mrs. Cheryl Darby of Cincinnati, Ohio, and Ms. Robin Bradley and Minister Bernadine Carruth of Massillon, Ohio, for their continual words of encouragement throughout this project.

introduction

REASONABLE expectations for black men of FAITH

from the very beginning of our lives, we live a life of expectation. We exit from our mother's womb expecting somebody to take care of our basic needs. We grow up expecting somebody to change our soiled diapers and to prepare our bottles. We attend school and expect somebody to help us with our homework. We become teenagers and expect somebody to purchase us the latest clothes and CDs.

Throughout our lives, we grow to expect many things from one another. Throughout our lives, we expect someone to be close by when we are in dire straits. Throughout our lives, we expect a friend to be a friend to the very end. Throughout our lives, we expect the good to outweigh and outwit the evil. Throughout our lives, we expect family members to watch our back when times get rough. Throughout our lives, we expect the marvelous light to overshadow the deception of the darkness. Throughout our lives, we expect our home team to bring home the victory. Throughout our lives, we expect peace to reign supreme over conflict. Throughout our lives, we expect God to give us the strength we need to hold on a little while longer. Throughout our lives, we expect more sunny days than cloudy nights. Throughout our lives, we expect the "effectual fervent prayers" of the righteous to "availeth much" (James 5:16) and for God to deal with our hurts and pains.

In the midst of all of our ups and downs, we are expected to keep a positive outlook, regardless of the volume, complexity, and extent of our trials and tribulations. We are expected to feel as Paul felt and say as Paul said, "Not that I speak in respect of want: for I have learned, in whatsoever state I am, therewith to be content. I know both how to be abased, and I know how to abound: every where and in all things I am instructed both to be full and to be hungry, both to abound and to suffer need. I can do all things through Christ which strengtheneth me" (Philippians 4:11-13). Paul goes on to say, "I have fought a good fight, I have finished my course, I have kept the faith: Henceforth there is laid up for me a crown of righteousness, which the Lord, the righteous judge, shall give me at that day: and not to me only, but unto all them also that love his appearing" (2 Timothy 4:7-8).

Paul had a positive attitude toward all of his trials and tribulations. And as the authors of this second edition of *Sound the Trumpet* illustrate, a positive attitude can increase our altitude in life. A positive attitude can help us, my brothers in Christ, to display more gratitude for how we have already been blessed! As the various sermons—all written for black men—emphasize, if we are to keep a positive outlook on life and live a life of promise and potential, we must live with one key ingredient—*faith!*

In all of the facets and stages of our lives as black men in America, we must possess faith, for without faith, it is impossible to please God. Without faith, it is impossible to trust God. Without faith, it is impossible to hear and listen to the voice of God. Without faith, it is impossible to believe that God has fully forgiven us of past transgressions. Without faith, it is impossible to believe that we are justified and set free from the bondage of sin, through the blood of our risen Savior. Without faith, it is impossible to forgive one another. Without faith, it is impossible to hold on to our sanity in the midst of persecution and character assassination. Without faith, it is impossible to tell mountains to move and demons to flee. Without faith, it is impossible to hold on to our dreams and hold out from compromising our principles. Without faith, it is impossible to believe the promises of God. Without faith, it is impossible to stay focused on the prize of the high calling of God in Christ Jesus, as opposed to the problem that we may be facing.

Sound the Trumpet Again! reminds us as Christian men that faith is needed—in this society and in our homes and in our souls—if we want to survive and thrive in this world. It goes without saying that faith is essential if you are going to try your hand at being a Christian. Faith is a necessary tool, weapon, and armor if you endeavor to live a life that is acceptable and pleasing before God! The authors remind us that faith is a discipline that we must have if we are going to believe that "The LORD is my light and my salvation; whom shall I fear? the LORD is the strength of my life; of whom shall I be afraid?" (Psalm 27:1). Faith in God Almighty is a must if we are going to believe that "The earth is the LORD's and the fullness thereof; the world, and they that dwell therein" (Psalm 24:1). Faith is required if we are going to believe Jesus when he said, "If ye abide in me, and my words abide in you, ye shall ask what ye will, and it shall be done unto you" (John 15:7).

You must have faith, brothers, if you are going to believe that "all things work together for good to them that love God, to them who are the called according to his purpose" (Romans 8:28). You must have faith if you are going to believe in a God that you can't see. You must have faith if you are going to believe in a God who will allow you to fall sometimes without breaking. You must have faith if you are going to serve a God who will allow you to cry sometimes in the midnight hour. You must have faith if you are going to follow a God who will allow a little rain to fall on the just as well as on the unjust. You must have faith if you are going to trust your life to a God whose Scriptures have declared, "Man that is born of a woman is of few days, and full of trouble" (Job 14:1). You must have faith if you are going to believe that the God you serve will never leave you nor forsake you. You must have faith if you are going to profess Jesus as your

Lord and Savior by confessing with your mouth that he is the Son of God, and he was raised from the dead on the third day.

We can expect a lot of things from God. But what can God expect from us? What does God expect from every man who calls himself a Christian? What can a majestic God who supplies all of our needs expect from his sons? In their own way, the preachers of the following sermons give us solid suggestions for what God is expecting from us as black men who strive to live a productive Christian life, full of dignity and integrity.

In the first five sermons, a theme will be apparent to readers. In their own way and right, these initial sermons speak to black men as servants of God in the context of the larger community. What are some reasonable expectations that God should have of black men as community leaders? These initial sermons show how God takes ordinary men and uses them to do extraordinary things! In the opening sermon, Charles G. Adams raises a poignant question: "Where Are the Men?" His major charge is for us to stand up as black men, to hear the voice of God, and to do what he bids us to do. On this same topic, Johnny Ray Youngblood asks us to consider which type of man we wish to be. In "Two Definitions of a Man," Youngblood juxtaposes the challenges men face as they endeavor to find their own identity and that which God calls them to be. In "How to Eradicate the Condition of 'Men-Who-Pause,'" using a play on words, Tyrone P. Jones IV beseeches us not to stand still, but rather to take action in fulfilling our divine purpose. In his eloquent way, Joe Samuel Ratliff, in "When Black Men Learn How to Beat the Blues," provides practical strategies on how to use the word of God to overcome trials and tribulations that are unique to black men. Lance Watson, in "Hands Full of Honey," reinforces the reality that struggles are inevitable and they come early in life but, with God in our lives, there will be sweet victories!

The next group of sermons address the reasonable expectations that God has for black men as fathers—to our own children and to future generations. These sermons do not give us an excuse to wallow in pools of pity or victimhood. Instead, the first three messages showcase that godly expectations exist for black fathers, despite the onslaught of social injustices so unique to black males in America. In "On Being a Black Father in America," J. Alfred Smith Sr. aggressively argues that black fathers cannot digest the pathological image the media portrays of black fathers. Using the work of Ralph Ellison, Smith urges us not to be invisible (or insignificant) in the lives of our children. Likewise, Rodney Maiden gives the non-negotiable declarative "Somebody Wake Up Daddy!" in his appropriately titled sermon. He bluntly illustrates what can happen to the men themselves, as well as to the community, church, and family, when black fathers rest in a Rip-Van-Winkle frame of mind. Then, Frank A. Thomas, focusing on God the Father, eloquently depicts how we must be about the Father's business. In "Thugs, Pretty Boys, and the Jesus Strategy," Thomas reminds us that, before we can be about the business of our Father God, we must acknowledge our role in being the "sons of the covenant."

In the next two sermons, the central theme is the responsibility of saving our current and future generations of black men. The authors address the issue of giving our sons the spiritual and racial identity they must have in order to survive in a country, in a democracy, that systematically creates barriers to their God-given potential. In "Saving Our Black Boys in America," Jim Holley exposes the social injustices facing our young men, and suggests ways to save them—and all of society—from these intentional demonic forces. In what is perhaps the most gut-wrenching title, "Kill Them Before They Grow," Claybon Lea Jr. takes a bold step in saying what few politically correct advocates dare to articulate: that there is compelling evidence that some people benefit from the destruction of our young black men, who represent the future of our people and our race. This exposé also offers solutions for change.

In the next group of sermons, the preachers share the overarching theme of self-empowerment. Rudolph McKissick Jr. draws upon the analogy of how today's society views black skin just as the biblical society viewed leprosy in "Don't Count Me Out!" Using a double entendre, he bluntly and passionately contends that we cannot let others define our identity for us, lest we adopt an inferiority identity and a sense of hopelessness and helplessness. Harold Hudson focuses on the metaphor of a fig tree in "From a Fruitless Life to a Fruitful Life." His sermon exhorts black men to live consistent and productive lives as Christians. Robert Charles Scott urges black men to have a vision and to share our voice. His sermon, "A Vision, a Voice, and an Adventure," admonishes us to remember that with a vision, we can see, and with a voice, we can be heard. With both a vision and a voice, black men can have a life that is a spiritual adventure! Gordon Humphrey Jr. also focuses on the notion adventure or journey. "Home for Good!" reminds us that many black men have lost their way for myriad reasons, but being lost does not have to be permanent, if we proactively set our vision on the Lord! Humphrey urges black men to remember the African proverb "it takes a village to raise a child." It also takes a village to help men who are lost to find their way home—for good!

This collection concludes with the core theme of self-identity within the context of reasonable expectations that God has of black men. In "The Courage to Be (Yourself)," Jamal-Harrison Bryant reminds us that we all have a personal I.D. given to us by the Lord. This unique I.D. must be our badge of honor—honor that should give us the courage to be who God wants us to be. Bryant shares with conviction the mandate that God wants us not to be afraid to be ourselves. Frederick "Freddie" D. Haynes

III shows us one of the means by which we as black men can actualize our identity. In his message to black men, "When God Hooks a Brother Up," he allows us to see how God truly intended for us to affirm our identity in the context of relationships within our culture. He uses a representative of the greatest group of people in creation: black women. Haynes illustrates masterfully how God used an African Egyptian sister to rejuvenate a brother's spirit and remind him of his divine role and purpose. He shows us that the sweetest and best honey to put in your "tea of life" is an African Honey.

Jeremiah A. Wright Jr. offers his praise for black men under the aptly titled sermon, "Thank God for Good Men!" With passion and persuasion, Wright challenges those who refuse to acknowledge the existence of good black men. He lays out several characteristics of Christian black men. This message is reinforced in "What Makes You So Great, Black Man?" by this book's editor, Darryl D. Sims. For black males—young and old alike—who do not know that they are great, the sermon tells them otherwise. For black males who do know that they are great, the sermon is a reminder, a spiritual booster shot, to give us an additional dose of positive racial identity.

It goes without saying that black men in America must fight negative stereotypes daily. However, it is time for us to take our campaign to the masses and stop crying foul. We can't expect anybody to do what is right in the sight of the Lord until we do what is right in the sight of the Lord. God has given us gifts and abilities that are second to none. There's nothing that we can't do for ourselves. We can build our own schools, fashion our own after-school programs, rebuild our own communities, and amass our own wealth. We can be self-sufficient and work together. Black man, step out on faith in God and step up to the plate of accountability. Be the strong man of divine color that you were created to be. We all need each other.

section one

TRUMPET SOUNDS to address
the SOCIAL ILLS of our day

chapter one

WHERE are the MEN?

Charles G. Adams

They heard the sound of the LORD God walking in the garden at the time of the evening breeze, and the man and his wife hid themselves from the presence of the LORD God among the trees of the garden. But the LORD God called to the man, and said to him, "Where are you?" He said, "I heard the sound of you in the garden, and I was afraid, because I was naked; and I hid myself."

He said, "Who told you that you were naked? Have you eaten from the tree of which I commanded you not to eat?" (Genesis 3:8-11, NRSV)

where are the men—particularly the black men, who are often referred to as "an endangered and quickly disappearing species"? The church, which is majority female, wants to know, Where are the men? The civil rights movement, gasping for breath and desperately in need of human help, wants to know, Where are the men? The NAACP, struggling to advance justice in the world, wants to know, Where are the men? Women, who find themselves outnumbering men more than two to one, want to know, Where are the men? A pastor, desperately in need of capable men to advance the church and to defend and develop the community, wants to know, Where are the men? And even God Almighty, walking to and fro throughout the world, wants to know, Where are the men? It was God, not a human being, who posed the question in the first place. The Bible is clear: if men are absent from society, it is only because they are first absent from God! It is because so many men have gone into seclusion, having hidden themselves from the presence of the Lord, that mortals find it necessary to ask, Where are the men?

Only when we are with God can we be humanly available to one another. But when we go far from God, we become absent, isolated, alienated, and separated from one another. If we are not here for God, we cannot be here for each other! If we do not love God, we cannot love each other! If we are not right with God, we cannot demonstrate integrity toward each other. If we are not thoroughly related to God, instructed by God's truth, corrected by God's word, energized by God's spirit, motivated by God's love, guided by God's hand, strengthened by God's power, saved by God's grace, we cannot be connected to the human family, to members of the church family, or be active in the continuing struggle to improve our common life. Surely, brothers, God is calling today. God's voice is echoing against the hard walls of our stone and stubborn resistance: Adam, where are you? Where are the men?

The question becomes critical when we consider that the word adam is a Hebrew word with two meanings—the generic meaning and the specific meaning. Generally speaking, adam is a generic term, an all-embracing term that means "man, mankind, or humankind." In that sense, God is speaking to everybody— male and female, occidental and oriental, east and west, south and north, young and old, rich and poor, Jew and Gentile, black and white—saying, "Humanity, where are you?"

The second meaning of the word adam in Hebrew is specific. It is a name, meaning Adam the man; the male Adam, the husband of Eve; Adam, the father of Cain and Abel; Adam, the primary ancestor of every race and nation; Adam, the progenitor of every human being; Adam, the first man in the human family; Adam, the common father of us all; Adam, whom God made an individual and placed in the Garden of Eden to develop it and maintain it.

The perennial question that faces us today is, "Where is Adam?" Adam is in the church, in the community, in the vortex of political strife, in the grassroots struggle against evil, in the rearing of children, in the support of the family, in the reconstructing of society, in the reordering and redeeming of human life. Adam, the person whom God made. Adam, the archetype of all people. Adam, where are you?

My brothers, something terrible and debilitating is happening to our sense of self and to our image of manhood. Something valuable is being lost in our unisex culture. And that something is the strong image, the clear conception, and the powerful presence of a wholehearted, true-hearted, stouthearted, level-headed, God-conscious, Christ-centered, church-oriented, spirit-intoxicated man. Something is especially wrong today in the image held of the African man, the black man, the first man that God ever made and appointed to be the archetype, the pattern, and the prototype of the human image of God. Where is the man? The voice of God is calling us to rise again, despite 385 years of this society's systematic rejection and disempowerment of the black male and female. Those who want to castigate and dominate the black race must dominate, emasculate, and eviscerate strong, self-assured, competent, and confident black men. We are a serious threat to the status quo. We are a formidable foe against racial injustice. We are convincing evidence against any theory of white supremacy!

The strong, capable black male (or female) never has been tolerated by Eurocentric society, never been allowed to come into his own. They suppressed W. E. B. Du Bois. They compromised Booker T. Washington. They excoriated Malcolm X. They murdered Medgar Evers. They persecuted Paul Robeson. They expelled Adam Clayton Powell Jr. They slandered Harold Washington. They smeared George Crockett. They slew Martin Luther

King Jr. They erased Max Robinson. They excommunicated Father Stallings. They discredited Manfred Byrd. They incarcerated Nelson Mandela. They killed Steve Biko. And they are impugning and ignoring forever any black male public figure because they realize that if they can dominate, debilitate, and devastate the strong black male and, thus, handicap the equally strong black woman, they can control and crush the race—step on our dreams, walk on our hopes, exploit our children, dominate our women, destroy our families, and murder our people.

And we are allowing them to do it. The first thing they have to do to get to our people is to get that black adult male out of the way. They have to get that strong, visible, viable, vocal, vibrant, vital, audible, stereotype-breaking man out of the way! And the tragedy is that we are helping them to do exactly that.

Some of us are pushing ourselves out of the way. We are parties to our own victimization and destruction! Dropping out when we ought to be hanging in. Cooling out when we ought to be digging in the books. Catching Z's when we ought to be making A's. Punching out when we ought to be pressing on. Hanging loose, staying aloof when we ought to be hanging together in Christ, in church, and in class. Lying down when we ought to be standing up. Shrinking back when we ought to be stepping forward. Vanishing out of sight when we ought to be visible and victorious.

My brothers, there is a conspiracy to exploit and destroy the black man and the black woman, the boy and the girl! But, it just will not happen—it cannot happen—if we stand up, be counted, and face the challenge of the hour!

Stand up, black male, and face the realities and opportunities of today! Stand up and see what is happening and what must be done in order for the human race to succeed and survive. Stand up and be sane, sensible, saved, and sanctified.

Black men, the 385-year-old conspiracy against our race is continuing. Our women are being exploited, and too many of us are allowing this to happen! It is not either/or. It is both/and. If they get the black man in the morning, they will get the black woman that night. So, either we will learn to love each other and hang together like sisters and brothers, husbands and wives, boyfriends and girlfriends, or we will surely hang separately and die tragically like fools. We either will survive together, or we will be destroyed separately.

Adam, where are you? The Middle Passage did not kill you. Slavery did not kill you. Jim Crow did not wipe you out. But now they have come up with something else to do away with you: a little, white, powdery poison designed to make you feel good and die young. I once attended the Black Family Community Conference on Crack Cocaine. This epochal meeting, convened by the Reverend Cecil Williams and the Glide Memorial United Methodist Church in San Francisco, attracted some 1,200 registered delegates. And I can say without fear or favor that it was the most important conference, convention, or meeting that I have ever attended because it examined and explained the greatest enemy ever to confront the African American community—crack cocaine.

We met to learn what we can do to win the war against crack because it dehumanizes its users. It devastates our communities. It destroys our culture, and it devitalizes our children. It destabilizes our families, and it deals death to our race. Not even slavery and segregation were as destructive of African American life and culture as crack cocaine. The use of this deadly drug renders its users totally isolated and alienated from their family and community. Crack cocaine culture is the nemesis, the antithesis, and death to black culture and traditional African American values.

Black culture, in its traditional form, promotes strong family values, encourages the pursuit of excellence, endorses a preference for spiritual over material values, mandates respect for elders and members of the opposite sex, advocates discipline to delay personal gratification in order to advance one's worthy aspirations, and generates concern for the well-being of the black race and the solidarity of the human race.

Drug culture, on the other hand, sponsors and encourages immediate gratification, destruction of family values, the pursuit of only hedonistic pleasure, preference for material values, total disregard and disrespect for elders and members of the opposite sex, no discipline to delay or control personal gratification, no concern for the progress of the black race or the condition of the human race. Crack cocaine destroys one's bonding with family, community, school, church, or indigenous African American culture. It is killing the entire race.

The conference emphasized that the black community has been especially targeted by the multinational drug cartels. Whole governments in Central and South America are being funded by profits on the sale of drugs to blacks in the United States. As jobs move out, drugs move in. Blacks are the highest risk group in the United States population.

Crack cocaine is intensely and immediately addictive. It is custom-made to destroy the black male. It is destructive of bodies, minds, and souls. It is extracted from the coca plant and mixed with baking soda. When heated, the substance can be liquefied or vaporized. It can be taken into the body by means of injection, snorting, or by inhalation. When injected, the drug's thrill is felt by the user in 20 seconds. When snorted, it comes in three minutes. When inhaled, the high comes in 10 seconds; then there comes a hard crash, deep depression, and psychological, physiological, and social dysfunction. After that comes a relentless, driving craving for more and more crack. That craving will blow all of the user's circuits. It actually destroys the body's natural reward and pleasure reactors. It throws the body and mind into disarray.

The crack addict lives only for crack. He or she is a slave to crack. Crack makes mothers destroy their children, makes children hate their parents, makes fathers forsake their families. It is a mean monster. It is a gigantic, terrible, awful destroyer, and it is keeping the black race down in fear, failure, and frustration. But if the black man would stand up, crack cocaine could be defeated.

Where is the black man? Come out of hiding. Where is Adam, the first man? When God called his name, he had gone into hiding. Overcome with the feeling of guilt and shame and the notion that he was unworthy and inferior because of moral failure, Adam hid himself behind the leaves of the fig tree. Many of us are hiding ourselves behind feelings of inferiority, self-denigration, self-deprecation, self-rejection, and self-hatred.

God asked, "Adam, where are you?" Adam said, "I am afraid because I'm naked; therefore I'm hiding." God asked, "Who told you that you were naked? Who told you I didn't make you right? Who told you I haven't already given you everything you need? Who told you that you are inferior? Who told you that you don't have a mind to think with, a heart to love with, eyes to see with, ears to hear with? Who told you that you lack anything that you have or need to have to be a complete person and to achieve greatly?" Black man, where are you? Who told you to go into hiding behind the leaves of self-abnegation? Who told you that you are inferior to anybody or anything?

The black race is inherently strong, resilient, and persistent. We have learned how to persevere. We have withstood more hardship and more systematic hatred and more cruelty and oppression than most people can imagine. We have been so exploited and rejected and denied and misused and abused that it is miraculous that we have not been wiped out completely and driven off the map! But, God made us a strong people! God gave us power to persevere, to endure, and to overcome.

The very pigment in our skin is a substance called melanin, and that is a sign of strength. It is a dominant trait and not a regressive characteristic. Whites do not have that rich brown melanin. They did not come to be in a climate where melanin was required to accommodate the relentless rays of the merciless sun. They do not have it. Therefore, it is a sign of weakness and deprivation. We have something they do not have and cannot get, no matter how much suntan lotion they use. So, in order to overcome their color deprivation, they have called what we have inferior, disgusting, and ugly, a sign of disgrace, of guilt, an emblem of shame and a mark of dishonor. Some of us have believed this lie and have become ashamed of the rich gift that God has given us, that is, our pigment, our melanin, our blackness. It is due to melanin, our distinctive and unique trait, that we can absorb the strong rays of the sun.

And that is not all. We have durable, darkened skin, and we have tough, motionless, obedient hair—hair that will lie down and stay where you put it until you move it. Do not call my hair "bad." I have good hair. It does not fall in my eyes. It does not fly in my face. It does not blow in my view. It does not obstruct my vision. It keeps going back, back, back out of the way so that it disappears rather than obstructing my work or blocking my progress.

And that is not all. We have strong straight backs. We can stand the sun. We can endure the heat. We can persevere under severe stress and mess. Of course, we can excel in sports, school, science, business, law, politics, and in everything else—if we are given a fair chance, and if we believe in ourselves! I've heard the saying, "No one can make you feel inferior without your consent."

My brothers, I am sad to say this, but we have gone into hiding. Instead of honoring and thanking God for our strength and our manhood and our melanin, we have been told that we have nothing, are nothing, and can do nothing. We have been taught to hate ourselves and to reject each other. Some black folks are ashamed to be who they are, and will make some white cosmetic company rich bleaching their skin, cooking and frying and baking and stewing their hair, straightening their noses, reducing their lips—all in an attempt to erase their African traits and cultural characteristics. We are hiding behind fig trees. It is disgusting to hear black folks say, "If you're white, you're all right. If you're yellow, you're mellow. If you're brown, stick around. If you are black, get back." That is disturbing and debilitating!

Brothers, we do not have to "get back" for anybody! We do not have to hide ourselves in shame. We are somebody! God made us in his own image. God has given us a wonderful gift. We are able to overcome the world because God is with us. We do not have to get back!

Black men, stop hiding! Stop hiding from others; stop hiding from yourself. Stop hating yourself. Stop running from yourself. Stop melting yourself into the melting pot. Stop merging yourself with the crowd. Stand up. Speak out. Step forward. Adam, where are you? Learn how to love yourself just like you are.

We have to stop hating ourselves! We have to start affirming ourselves. We ought to get up every morning and affirm ourselves. Look in the mirror and say, "I thank God for me. I love me, because God made me, Jesus saved me, the Holy Ghost anointed me, mercy found me, love lifted me, goodness and mercy shall follow me all the days of my life, and I shall dwell in the house of the Lord forever."

We are a strong people spiritually! The only people on earth who ever gave the world a religion are nonwhite Asians and Africans. The oldest religion in the world came out of Egypt, which is in Africa. Not one of the world religions came out of Europe, but were taken to Europe by African missionaries. The oldest existing Christian church is located in Abyssinia, Ethiopia. The greatest church fathers and theologians are black people— Augustine, Tertullian, and Cyprian. It was nonwhite people, dark-skinned people who gave the world the Bible, taught the world what the name of God is Yahweh (the divine tetragammaton,

YHWH, mistakenly referred to as Jehovah by people who don't know Hebrew), and that God is fully present in Jesus Christ.

We are a strong people—spiritually, ethically, legalistically, artistically. We can listen to the whispering winds of eternity, and then put the message down on paper. While some people who do not know history argue over whether the Roman Catholic Church can stand to be ruled by a black pope, we know that already history records three black popes in the remote past. They were St. Victor I (189–199), St. Miltiades (311–314), and St. Gelasius I (492–496).[1]

My uncle, the late Gordon Blaine Hancock, published an article in the *Journal of Negro History* in 1921 entitled "The Three Elements of African Culture." He argued that we had the basic elements of "high culture" long before we ever came in contact with whites from Europe. We had the three necessary elements: religion, art, and law.

Chancellor Williams of Howard University said the same thing in *Destruction of Black Civilizations*. G. M. James said the same thing in *Stolen Legacy*, namely that European technology is rooted in African intelligence; that Greek philosophy is the flower of Ethiopian wisdom; that Beethoven's *Ninth* is a variation of an African musical theme; that Dvorak's *New World Symphony* is but the improvisation of a black musical creation; that civilization was perfected in Africa when Europeans were running around half-naked behind trees in the woods of Britain, France, and Germany.

We are a strong people. We are a blessed race! Our strength is meant to keep us independent of those who would define us and rule over us. But Adam, you have to come out of hiding. You must stop hating yourself. You must stop being counterfeit!

Where is the black man? Hiding! Therefore, he is out of touch with his true self. The only way to know who you are is to know who God is! And the only way to be who you are is to be in agreement with God. The only way to get in touch with yourself is to get in contact with the God who made you.

Black man, come out of hiding. Get in touch with who you are. Develop the man God made you to be. Don't let anybody make you anything that you are not. Who told you that you were inferior to anybody? Ah, but there's another side to that question. Who told you that you were superior to women? In Genesis 1, man and woman are made together in one act of creation. In Genesis 2, God brings one woman out of the side of one man. But the message in both Genesis 1 and Genesis 2 are that male and female are equal. That's the message: We don't have to put her down to lift ourselves up, because she was not made from our hands to be manipulated by us; she was not made from our feet to be trampled by us; she was not made from our elbow to be elbowed out by us; she was not made from our fist to be beat up on by us; she was not made from our back to lag behind us. She was made from our side to walk beside us, in dignity, equality, and integrity. So don't abuse women. You are not a man because you can beat up on a woman. You are a man because you know how to love a woman. You are not a man because you can make a baby. You are a man if you know how to rear a child.

The whole world is waiting for you, my brothers! The whole world needs your ministry and your consecration. Martin Luther King Jr. taught us that the whole world is bound together in a single bundle of destiny. So whatever affects one group affects every other group. You can't have nuclear disaster in Russia and breathe clean air in the United States! The relentless wind blows remote disasters into your comfortable parlors. Injustice anywhere is a threat to people everywhere. Disease anywhere is a danger to health everywhere. Poverty anywhere is a mirror of greed everywhere. Dope addiction anywhere diminishes sobriety and sanity everywhere. One group cannot rise and leave others wallowing in the gutter of denial.

Everybody has lost ground. We all need to win some battles. Stand up, black man! What are you going to do about the fact that our neighborhoods are being destroyed by dope? What are you going to do about the fact that our children are being equipped with guns, but not an education? What are you going to do about the fact that jobs are being lost in the United States, and they are being transplanted to China, Korea, Mexico, and South Africa where wages are cheap? What are you going to do about the fact that 50 percent of blacks, age twenty-one to sixty-five, are functionally illiterate; 30 percent of blacks are unemployed; 50 percent of blacks are high school dropouts; 20 percent of blacks are hooked on dope; 35 percent of blacks don't belong to anything—not the Elks, the Masons, the PTA, the NAACP, the block club, or the church? Black babies are eight times more likely to get AIDS, five times more likely to land in prison, and ten times more likely to die before they've had a chance to live.

Black man, stand up! We know what you can do if you really want to do it. Hear the voice of God, and answer to your name. Stand up, African American man! Liberate your people. If you don't stand up, the church will be debilitated; the community will be devastated; the school will be dominated; the world will be disintegrated; your children will be truncated; the race will be apocopated! Stand up, black man—glorify the Lord, gratify the race, fortify the people, rectify the wrong, purify the community, sanctify the family, satisfy the need, qualify the children, and glorify God.

Stand up, black man! If it can be done, you can do it. If there is a problem, you can solve it. If there is a cancer, you can cure it. If there is a misunderstanding, you can drop it. If there is hatred, you can shake it. If there is trouble, you can take it. If there is a mountain, you can move it. If there is a battle, you can fight it. If there is prejudice, you can overcome it. If there is a cross, you can bear it. If there is a challenge, you can face it. If they knock you down, you can get up. If they push you against the ropes, you can come out swinging. If they kill you, you can rise again!

Stand up! Stand up, black man! You are not inferior. You are a child of God, made in God's image, washed in the blood of Jesus, sanctified by the Holy Ghost. "No weapon that is fashioned against you shall prosper" (Isaiah 54:17). "God did not give us a spirit of cowardice, but rather a spirit of power and of love and of self-discipline" (2 Timothy 1:7).

Stand up! Face the battle. Fight the fight. Do the work. Win the victory! Adam, where are you?

NOTE

1. *Cited by Randal Robinson in* The Debt *(New York: Penguin Putnam, Inc., 2000), 18.*

chapter two

TWO DEFINITIONS of a man

Johnny Ray Youngblood

And he stood and cried unto the armies of Israel, and said
unto them, ... choose you a man for you, and let him come
down to me. If he be able to fight with me, and to kill me,
then will we be your servants: but if I prevail against him,
and kill him, then shall ye be our servants, and serve us. And
the Philistine said, I defy the armies of Israel this day; give
me a man, that we may fight together. (1 Samuel 17:8-10)

And I sought for a man among them, that should make up
the hedge, and stand in the gap before me for the land, that
I should not destroy it: but I found none. (Ezekiel 22:30)

in an effort to make these texts come alive, i'd
like for us to imagine both of these passages, 1 Samuel 17:8-10
and Ezekiel 22:30, as classified ads in the *Sunday Times*—in the
"Help Needed" section. Then, these passages would read a little
bit like this.

Man needed to make up the hedge and to stand in the gap
before God so the land and country won't be destroyed.
Apply immediately. (Ezekiel 22)

Nation in trouble—under threat of enemy! Man needed to
fight and kill enemy mascot. If applicant succeeds, Israel will
be served. If applicant fails, Israel will serve. (1 Samuel 17)

Brethren, if you or I were alive at the time that these ads were
placed in the *Times*, who of us this morning would apply? Who
of us will qualify if we did apply?

I tremble to think that the Ezekiel ad would reach the same conclusion: "… but I found none." I dare say that 1 Samuel 17 would run for days, because most of us would cower or disqualify ourselves at the thought of fighting Goliath! However, I make bold to tell you that, although the original parchments on which the want ads were penned have yellowed and faded and are at risk from the slightest gust of wind, a new edition has been published and these want ads are being run again today: MAN NEEDED!

But lest I lead you the wrong way, I better say that only one position is still open; only one ad is still being run, and that is 1 Samuel 17. The Ezekiel 22 position has been filled. It took a while, but it was filled! A number of folk applied and most did not qualify, but the position finally got filled! Abraham applied, but his misleading tongue and his avaricious spirit disqualified him; Isaiah applied, but his unclean lips and his blinding stare at Uzziah disqualified him; Isaac applied, but his wells were deeper than his faith; David applied, but like Moses, his blood-stained hands disqualified him; Jeremiah applied, but he cried too much; Ezekiel himself applied, but he didn't really live in the real world. So God, who placed the ad in the first place, said, "I'll do it myself. I'll qualify myself for the job, and do it myself!" And, he did, in the person of Jesus of Nazareth, the Christ. (Now, although that specific position has been filled, another want ad now takes its place. And that is, "Men needed to recruit men, to walk through the gap that has been filled and to hide behind the hedge that's been made up.")

But the position for 1 Samuel 17 is still open. Read the ad again, my brothers: "Nation in trouble—under threat of enemy. Man needed to fight and kill the enemy mascot. If applicant succeeds, Israel will be served. If applicant fails, Israel will serve." Let's bring the ad up to date: "Black folk in trouble—under threat of enemy. Man needed to fight and kill the enemy mascot. If applicant succeeds, black folk will be served. If applicant fails, black folk shall continue to serve."

What we need to notice about these biblical texts is that these two passages have the same cry: MAN WANTED! MAN WANTED! From two different sources, the cry comes, MAN WANTED! And for two different reasons, the cry comes, MAN WANTED! The cry is, "I'm looking for a man."

Notice the two voices that announce the search, that make the appeal. In Ezekiel 22 the voice is God himself. God says, "I'm looking for a man." 1 Samuel 17 quotes Goliath of Gath. He says, "I'm looking for a man." Both of these voices—God and Goliath—are entities of size and power. Some of us know God. Not all of us, but some of us, know him. Some of us have received the grace to know God. Some of us are the recipients of the grace to see God. Some of us are the recipients of the grace to hear God, and many of us are recipients of the grace to experience God.

Brothers, do you know God Almighty? If you don't, let me just tell you a couple of things about him. God is the one who originates life; God is the one who terminates life; God is the one who washes the air with his rain and who sweeps the earth with his wind. Brothers, God laid the grass like a carpet and then tacked it down with flowers. God is the one who calls for our attention when he orchestrates the roll of the thunder's bass drum, and he counters it with the cymbals of his lightning.... God, do you know him? He is the architect and designer of all things wild and wonderful. God is the designer of creatures great and small. God is the architect of all things grand and glorious. The bottom line is that anything that has been made was made by God. Brothers, God is the one who put strength in the mountains, who gave height to the pine, who makes sturdy the oak. God is the one who put the wet in water and the dry in sand, who put heat in the fire and put cold in the ice.

God didn't quit there. The Lord painted the robins red and the elephants grey, the sky blue and the grass green. God painted me and you black, these folks white, those ones yellow, those ones red, and if there's really anybody on Mars, he made them green.

God is alive and well. And, brothers, what we need to know is that God is looking for a man! Extra, extra! Read all about it! God is looking for a man!

Now, Goliath was not God. He had size—he was nine feet tall—but he was a freak, with possibly four brothers who were also of intimidating height. He had a voice like the bottom of a well. He had the strength of at least ten men—he wore approximately 1,200 pounds of armor for battle. But, he wasn't God.

God and Goliath: two different beings, but both of them looking for a man. God needs a man to stand before him and Goliath. The land is under threat. Children's futures are not bright. The presence of men and women are on the brink. But a man can save the day! A man can stabilize the present and secure the future! Don't you hear the call reverberating throughout history? MAN WANTED. MAN WANTED. MAN WANTED.

Well, we know the need and we know the assignment, but what are the qualifications? I'm glad you asked that question. If we look at 1 Samuel 17, we sense that, really, there are two definitions of a man. Goliath had one definition, and God had one definition. Goliath was looking for a male with physical size and muscular power. Goliath was looking for a man who was a victim of patriotic fever and a man who possessed some military genius.

I think Goliath has influenced us more than we realize when it comes to our definition of A MAN. We think a man is always one who has the height of Ed Lawson, so men who fall short feel they have to make up for their lack of height. They act out of what's called a "napoleonic complex." (Napoleon was a short man who compensated for his stature by trying to conquer all of Europe.) Goliath has affected a whole lot of us. And if you don't believe me, just think about some of our definitions of A MAN: tall, dark, rugged, heroic, powerful. If he's a man, he can push folk around. If a male is soft and loving, somebody says he's a sissy. Goliath has influenced us more than we realize.

Goliath didn't just have size; he had weapons also. Goliath felt that A MAN is a guy who has weapons to fight with, to do war in life. And most of us predicate our manhood on our weapons. Goliath had a shield in front of him, and his shield was so large he had to have somebody else carry his shield. His sword was so long that when David killed him, David had to use both hands to wield it. Goliath's breastplate was so large that it weighed somewhere in the vicinity of 125 pounds.

Now, we don't have swords and shields and breastplates like Goliath, but we've got weapons. And you know something? We think our weapons make us men. We've got cars; we think, the bigger our car, the bigger men we are. We figure the better our clothes, the better men we are. We figure the more money we have, the more we can flash. I saw a brother walk past me one Sunday with a wad of money that would choke three horses at Aqueduct. At offering time, he walked around the sanctuary, and when he got to the front, he pulled out his money, looked up at me, peeled off a dollar, and gave it to God. I've heard ladies talk about how they watch how, when a man wants to get with them, what he'll do is pull out his money and flash it. You know, like "Hey baby ... ah, you know." Come on, brothers, you know what I'm talking about. And all I'm trying to say is that Goliath has given us our definition of A MAN.

We've got other weapons, like our sexual prowess! And then we've got, especially here in New York, con artistry. This con game is a weapon that men use. We are constantly taking on weapons in order to protect us against the darts and arrows of life. Goliath has affected us. If we don't have money, a lot of us feel our manhood is endangered. When we get up in age and when our sexual prowess fades, we start to feel that life is over. When our car is down, we feel that we can't go anywhere. If we have no job, we get so depressed that we can't even go out and look for another one.

And Goliath is still saying, "Give me a man." He's got criteria that he wants us to live up to that we'll never achieve—not when it comes down to Goliath's definition of A MAN. There will always be somebody stronger than you; there will be somebody with a bigger sword and a larger breastplate; somebody with a better track record than you, and so, if you go by Goliath's definition, you will never be A MAN. And brothers, what you've got to know about Goliath is that he knew there was nobody in Israel his size. That's why he was out there selling those "giant tickets." He knew there was nobody in Israel his size. Nobody would fit his definition of A MAN, because his definition was limited and limiting.

Brothers, you know the people of God are still attacked and ridiculed about the absence of men and the inability of the men who *are* present to achieve. "What are the men doing in the church?" folk will ask. "Where are the men in church? Ain't no men in church." Or, if they really want to cut at us, they'll sneer, "Ain't no *real* men in church."

It's not only bad when Goliath sells these giant tickets that we can't buy. What's worse is when we *do* buy Goliath's definition of A MAN! Brothers, there are folk who will tell us that being a man is what Goliath is calling for, and I want to serve notice that Goliath's definition is *not* the essence of being a man. Physical strength has nothing to do with it. A man is not defined by his size. I've been told, "It ain't the size of the ship, it's the motion of the ocean!" Somebody else said, "It's not the wand, it's the magician!" I submit to you that a man is one who knows how to get up and try again. A man is one who never allows anybody to get over on him.

Brothers, we've got the wrong criteria for manhood! We've been given the wrong job description. We've been given the wrong advertisement. And many of us have been given the wrong training and preparation. And when we buy Goliath's definition of A MAN, we always sell ourselves short. What we need to know is that, while Goliath was taunting Israel, Goliath was the real fool. What he failed to remember was that, even if he thought there was no man in Israel who lived up to his standards, there was (and is!) a God in Israel. And because God is in Israel, he hears what you say and he sees what you do. And God will not allow his own to be put to shame indefinitely. Goliath wanted a man, and I'm glad to announce that when Goliath cried for A MAN, especially from Israel, God provided a man!

Now Saul, who was the king, had been brainwashed into accepting Goliath's definition of A MAN, so Saul looked over the man God handed him. But, my brothers, God *had* a man. Ain't that good news? When the enemy of God's people was looking for A MAN, there was no man according to the enemy's calculations. But God did have a man there! This man was not as old as Goliath, but he was a man. In fact, he wasn't old enough even to be drafted into the Israelite army, but he was a man. He wasn't nine feet tall—he probably stood between four and five feet—but he was a man. He was not skilled in military warfare; all he could really do was play a harp, write poetry, and swing a mean sling, but he was a man. He was not adorned with the protective armor of war; he just dressed himself in a shepherd's clothes, but he was a man! He held no position in the nation, just the youngest son of a man named of Jesse, but he was God's man!

David was God's man to save the nation. He was provided and prepared for battle by God. God looked over Eliab and Shammah and the other brothers of David. They had size; they were eligible for the draft; they had military prowess. But they were not the men God wanted to defend his people.

David was a young shepherd boy. David was out in the plains of Bethlehem, probably with his sandals filthy most of the time and mud between his toes. He carried a shepherd's staff. His hair was disheveled. His skin was dark from being baked by the noon-day sun. Then, when Goliath called for a man, God heard him and God sent a man. God chose David. Now, Goliath thought he was a boy, but God knew he was a man. David confronted Goliath, and David won the battle. David cut off Goliath's head. David saved the Israelite army.

Black men, consider David's qualifications for the job at hand. First, David had pride in his people. David loved Israel, and *one of the things we need now is men who love black folk*. We need black men who love their own. Brethren, I know it seems like nothing, but we need to stop making jokes about ourselves. It's all right to laugh at ourselves, but we've got to stop putting ourselves down with jokes because this has made us selfish and every man now looks out for himself. But today, as a man of God, I'm saying that we've got to lift our vision and concern, even beyond our immediate family, and see the need of black people in this nation.

I don't have to tell you that our nation, our community, is threatened; you see this for yourself. Genocide is a definite reality! The modern-day Goliath is more sophisticated. This new and stealthy Goliath is defying A MAN to come forth. And God is looking for a man to answer that challenge. Martin Luther King came forth and this new Goliath killed him, but Martin was still God's man because he took more out of Goliath than Goliath knew he had to lose.

God is still looking for a man! This new Goliath is preventing a lot of men from coming forth by the unfair and discriminatory laws that are being passed on a daily basis. This new Goliath is sifting the pride and strength out of a lot of our men. This new Goliath is creating obstacles and planting traps in new places to lure us away from the mandates of God. This new Goliath orchestrates circumstances that make it difficult for us as black men to be more involved in our communities. However, God is still looking for a man. Brothers, like David we must take pride in our community!

The second thing, men, is that *we have to feel good about ourselves*. One of the illnesses I've discovered is low self-esteem. Too many men I know don't feel good about themselves. That's the reason so many of our brothers are on drugs—because they don't like themselves. If you loved yourself, you would not pop pills into that strong, beautiful, black body of yours. If you loved yourself, you wouldn't stick those needles in your arms and legs. If you loved yourself, you wouldn't drink the liquor that folk from another area code push in your community. If you really loved yourself, you would take pride in yourself, you would learn how to talk, you would learn how to treat others, and you would learn how to treat yourself.

David felt good about himself and he said, "Well, I don't know if I can beat this fellow, but I'm sure going to give it a hell of a try!" Some of us are defeated before we even try, and that's because we don't like ourselves. I'm not telling you to become narcissistic, where you just think you're the only one in the world, but you've got to love yourself before you can love your neighbor. I know this because Jesus told us so. Jesus said, "Love your neighbor as you love yourself."

So first, we need to care about our community, about our people. Second, we need to feel good about and love ourselves. And, third, *we need to trust God*. David trusted in God. David saw that his height was different from Goliath's. David knew that his biceps and triceps would not measure up to Goliath's. David tried on Saul's armor, but the armor was too big. Men, this means you've got to be yourself! You can't try to be like somebody else. You have to be yourself. If David had gone out in Saul's armor, he would have lost the battle. He would have tripped over Saul's sword. The breastplate would have hung too low and probably beat his knee caps to death. His helmet would have fallen over his eyes. David had to be himself and use what he had.

So, David did what he knew he had to do, with what he had to do it with, in the name of the Lord. Yes, he did! The record tells me that David said, "I can't let this go.... I'm going to fight this fight with what the Lord has provided!" Then he walked down through the valley. There was a stream running down that mountain, and he went down by the brook and picked up five smooth stones. He used only one on Goliath, but he knew that Goliath had four brothers, and David had enough sense to know that if he killed Goliath, the giants would keep on coming. So he was ready, just in case the enemy was planning to live up to his reputation. David walked down through that valley concentrating on the divine presence, and I can hear him saying, "Yea, though I walk through the valley of the shadow of death I will fear no evil; for thou art with me."

David was on his way down there, but his brothers were saying "Don't go." Brethren, you need to know that some of your brothers are scared; some of your brothers won't let you be the man that you ought to be! They're afraid for themselves and they're afraid for you, but when you're in touch with the Lord, even when your brothers are scared, you walk anyway. You may be afraid, but while you're walking, you know that you're not by yourself. Just say those comforting words, "The Lord is my shepherd, and I shall not want."

David went down there. I see him in my mind's eye, grabbing his slingshot, laying it out, reaching into his shepherd's bag, pulling out one of those smooth stones, and putting it in that slingshot. I can see him pulling the two ends together, getting ready to wind it up. I can see David as he winds it up. I see him right now, as he winds it the first time. And I see him praying right quick as he twirls it a second time. "Renew my strength," he prays as he swings it one last time, and then he lets it go!

My brothers in Christ, when you are God's man, you're never by yourself. Even nature worked on David's behalf. That rock left the slingshot, and then one of the angels that controls the wind let a gust of wind go, and the rock struck Goliath's forehead, dead center. I can hear David saying, "Thou preparest a table before me, in the presence of mine enemies." I see him after he gained the victory and returned home; everybody wants his autograph. I see David signing autographs and saying, "Fret not thyself because of evil doers, neither be thou envious against the workers of iniquity, for they shall soon be cut off and wither away as the green grass." I see him writing poetry again: "He that dwelleth in the secret place of the Most High shall abide under the shadow of the Almighty." Listen to David declare, "I will say of the Lord, he is my refuge and my fortress; my God, in him will I trust."

Well, my brothers, God is looking for a man! I am just a recruiter. The army needs somebody. We are soldiers in the army. We've got to fight. And although we have to cry, we've got to hold up the blood-stained banner. We've got to hold it up until we die.

Goliath has one definition of manhood, but God has another definition. Brothers, we must stand and walk through the gap! Jesus paid the toll. At the cross, Jesus paid it all. Sin left a crimson stain, but Jesus washed it. Oh, my brother, whatever your name is, whatever your deeds are, Jesus is looking for you! You don't have to be perfect to come in. He says, "Come as you are, and let me tell you what I'll do. I'll give you strength for your weakness, joy for your sorrow, hope for your despair, light for your darkness, salvation for your damnation, and peace for your confusion." I have one witness that I need to call on right now. The apostle Paul said, "If any man be in Christ, he is a new creature: old things are passed away; behold, all things are become new" (2 Corinthians 5:17).

I'm a new man in Christ! God is looking for a man. God is looking for a man. Although your sins be crimson, he'll wash them. The Lord needs somebody. Brothers, we all have to answer this ad one glorious morning. You ought to come, black men, and give your life to Jesus Christ!

chapter three
how to ERADICATE the condition of "men-who-pause"
Tyrone P. Jones IV

And the Philistine said, I defy the armies of Israel this day; give me a man, that we may fight together. When Saul and all Israel heard those words of the Philistine, they were dismayed, and greatly afraid. (1 Samuel 17:10-11)

i do not in any way mean to make light of the transitory condition that women experience through what is known as menopause. I do, however, through the play on words in my title, wish to make the argument that this condition of arrested development can also be seen through the actions of some men. No, I am not a gynecologist nor am I one who works in internal medicine, but through my limited understanding of the menopausal condition, I have come to know certain things. When women experience menopause, it means that they are no longer able to produce life because of the shutdown of the menstrual cycle, and due to this shutdown, some women experience symptoms connected to this change in their bodies.

As I look at the condition of some of men, I find that our external actions mirror the internal conditions of woman who suffer from menopause. In reference to this analogy, I believe that the full potential in some men has diminished because of the circumstances they are facing. It is disheartening to see that young men who should be enjoying dreams of grandeur, instead are having thoughts of suicide as their way of escape. Furthermore, too many of us are motivated by the crippling mindset of "survival of the moment." I have found that the conflict within black men that stops the flow of life toward reaching one's potential is *fear*.

Fear will stunt your growth by cutting you off from your flow of creative juices and innovative strategies. The flow that I speak about is the blood that comes from a man's soul. It is necessary for this purpose-driven flow to continue in order to reach one's fullest potential. The condition of "men-who-pause" can keep men awestruck, preventing us from receiving adequate attention in our time of need. Here are what I believe to be the top five symptoms of the condition I call men-who-pause:

1. Men-who-pause keeps a man who needs medical attention from seeking early detection from various forms of cancer and disease.
2. Men-who-pause keeps a high-school dropout from going back to school, and a high-school graduate from going forward and getting a good quality education.
3. Men-who-pause keeps a brother who lives in the ghetto from experiencing a broader sense of the world outside of the ghetto.
4. Men-who-pause keeps a man from committing to an intimate relationship with a woman and with their children.
5. Men-who-pause keeps a man who is seeking employment from finding employment, and as a result, that brother is mis-labeled as "lazy, trifling, and good for nothing."

African-American brothers, men-who-pause is a serious condition that causes severe trauma due to overexposure of the mind to negative situations. But I know a God who can intercede and bring peace in the midst of all of our problems!

At the time of our text, the people of Israel had a serious problem. The problem was in what lay ahead of them, for Israel was engaged in battle with what would seem to be an unconquerable nemesis. The Philistines were an archenemy who had plagued Israel and taunted them for some time. The record is that both armies drew their battle lines on adjacent hills facing each other.

The Israelites were on one side and the Philistines were on the other side, with the valley of Elah between them. This classic military strategy would seem like the perfect opportunity for Israel to engage wholeheartedly in battle, but something in particular caused the men of Israel to experience great trepidation in moving toward their victory. The Bible tells us that a champion from Gath, named Goliath, stood up and defied all the armies of Israel. Verse 16 records that this Philistine giant named Goliath taunted Israel for forty days and nights. Israel was supposed to be the army under God; Israel was supposed to be ready for battle; Israel was supposed to be poised for prominence. Yet, they did not have the faith to act on what they represented as a nation.

In like manner, our nation of black men has become susceptible to overcoming the giants of our modern-day dilemmas. Brothers, we are supposed to be the generation of men who stand up in times of difficulty, rather than freeze in fear or falter in failure or take flight when it is time to fight. Black men who are in this condition suffer from what I call men-who-pause. They have disrobed themselves of the spirit of grit and determination, and they have placed upon themselves the spirit of lethargy, putting on the mantel of do-nothingness. These are they who speak with confidence, but act in cowardice. These are they who will say "I'm standing on the promises," but at the first sign of trouble, they run from believing in the promises.

The condition of men-who-pause starts in the heart of men and works its way through the body to affect the upper and lower extremities. In other words, if you are not careful, men-who-pause will cause your feet to stand still and your hands to fall limp in a time of battle. It will prevent you from expecting a change to come, and it will prevent you from believing in miracles. It will cause you to become immersed in mediocrity. It will cause you to settle for the status quo. It will cause you to continue mere business as usual. It will prevent you from looking beyond where you currently are, and it will cause you to accept defeat at the hands of your enemies, without rendering a fight.

So, I have come to talk to the brothers who, for far too long, have suffered in silence. I've come to tell the brothers who are in need of a breakthrough that your liberation will come—because when you *speak up and speak out,* then you can *stand up and stand out.* To *speak up* means you get the attention of your condition. To *speak out* means you speak with authority so you can be recognized. To *stand up* means you move forward without any hint of fear. To *stand out* means you exemplify excellence from within!

In Israel's case, their silence gave way to fear. Verse 24 says that when they saw the giant, "they fled, consumed with fear." Fear is a compounded condition that causes the symptoms of men-who-pause to get worse. But what I love about God is that he always has a remedy for whatever ails us. We have to realize that the threat and condition that confronts us is an opportunity for God to work through us!

When David appeared on the scene, he came to see about his brothers on the front lines of war, but what he found was the broken spirit of men who had been violently infected with the disease of men-who-pause. So David began to speak up and speak out. Look at verse 26:

> And David spake to the men that stood by him, saying, What shall be done to the man that killeth this Philistine, and taketh away the reproach from Israel? for who is this uncircumcised Philistine, that he should defy the armies of the living God?

David's resolve was unwavering; he had determined in his mind that he was not going to let the Philistines—or any army for that matter—defy his God or his people. My brothers, if we are going to eradicate the sickness of men-who-pause, we have to first tell ourselves, "I will no longer be intimidated by the debilitating tactics of the enemy." Now, when you do this, there will be those who are close to you who will remind you of where you are and who they know you to be. Look at verse 28:

> And Eliab his eldest brother heard when he spake unto the men; and Eliab's anger was kindled against David, and he said, Why camest thou down hither? and with whom hast thou left those few sheep in the wilderness? I know thy pride, and the naughtiness of thine heart; for thou art come down that thou mightest see the battle.

A lot of times, when you speak in advance of something happening, people will mistake your confidence for arrogance, but all you're doing is saying, "Any way that the Lord decides to bless me, I know I will be satisfied!" To combat that divine confidence, what the enemy will do is use the likes of those who are close to you to remind you of where you are right now. But because they are so close to you, they are too close to see where you are going in the future! That's why the devil likes to remind us of where we are now, because—guess what? The enemy has no hold on our future.

So after David spoke up and spoke out, he had to stand up so he could stand out. The Bible says that David kept speaking to the men. He asked in verse 29, "Is there not a cause?" and while he was yet speaking, Saul summoned him. When he came before Saul, David stood up and said in verse 32, "Let no man's heart fail because of him (Goliath); your servant will go and fight with this Philistine."

Know that there will be those who will tell you that you are not qualified to do the job, but that is when you have to show them that the words that you speak are guaranteed by your faith. David had to show Saul some personal references, so he dug out his faith file and under the letter B, he told Saul how he had fought a bear for the sake of the sheep, and under the letter L, he described how he fought a lion and rescued the lambs. Then David told Saul, "I have confidence that God will deliver us from our enemies."

This is how you stand up—by trusting in the power that is beyond your realm of comprehension. In other words, you don't know how God does it; all you know is that *he does it!* So when you stand up against the condition of men-who-pause, you demonstrate through faith the power to persevere because you know that this condition is now temporary at best. And I believe that when you stand up, that's when God will move.

Brothers, one thing I love about God is that, if you are faithful to him, he will be faithful to you. I don't care what the situation looks like. My expectations in the Lord help me to see clearly out of my bad situation. Hebrews 11:6 tells us, "But without faith it is impossible to please him: for he that cometh to God must believe that he is, and that he is a rewarder of them that diligently seek him."

David stood out because, even in the midst of doubt and disagreement from the others, he was willing to lay it all on the line. In verse 45, David said to Goliath himself, "Then said David to the Philistine, Thou comest to me with a sword, and with a spear, and with a shield: but I come to thee in the name of the LORD of hosts, the God of the armies of Israel, whom thou hast defied." Verse 46 says, "This day will the LORD deliver thee into mine hand; and I will smite thee, and take thine head from thee; …" This discourse from David gives us a glimpse into just how radical we have to become in order to combat the radical nature of men-who-pause. It takes a radical belief to eradicate a radical condition!

When a snake bites you, the poison can ultimately lead to death, but the antidote to save you derives from the same toxin that had the power to kill you. In other words, when you have been struck by a debilitating blow from the enemy, the same intensity that the devil uses against you is the same intensity you are going to need to destroy him! Some of us remain sick for lack of a radical disposition. We want to get healed, but God wants not only to heal us physically but also to heal us mentally and spiritually.

You know, another reason David was able to stand out was because of the divinity of God that was in him. He knew that the divine nature of God was mirrored in the divine nature within him. So, not only did David speak with the same intensity as the enemy, but he also spoke clearly the words that represented who God was and what God was able to do. In common language, David spoke so that the divinity in him could connect with the divinity in God. My brothers, we need to realize that when we accept the Lord as our Savior, then we all have the divine nature of God within us! Now, I'm not talking about just the Spirit of God directly, but I'm talking about what the Spirit of God deposits in us as an alternative to sin.

The Spirit of God is what nurtures us, and the by-product of that nurture from God's Spirit is the residue of God's divine nature. For instance, when you pour Liquid Drano in your sink, the residue of the liquid substance remains behind in order to clear out all of your pipes. The residue of the Spirit of God (God's divine nature) is what is left behind as a change agent to combat all of your problems. David was short in stature, but he was big in courage because of the spiritual substance that was inside of him! Inside of you, there is a spiritual tiger waiting to get out. God has given us a spiritual elastic band, which means we can handle more stuff because God has given us the stamina to stand out.

Finally, David had to survive this ordeal because God's reputation was on the line! When you stand up and stand out for God, then God is now obligated to intercede on your behalf. God is obligated not only because your neck is on the line, but also because his own reputation is on the line.

How would it look if God could not provide? How would it look if God could not heal? How would it look if God could not protect? How would it look if God could not speak something out of nothing? How would it look if God could not be our banner in a time of war? How would it look if God could not be our shepherd so we need not want? How would it look if God could not forgive our sins? How would it look if God could not be our light and our salvation? How would it look if God could not be our bread when we are hungry? How would it look if God could not be our friend when we feel friendless?

I know that God wants to keep his reputation intact because God's reputation brings about a sense of expectation for him to respond. Often, God is the only one who can respond to the giants that enter our lives to destroy us!

I know that the terrain of this biblical text about David versus Goliath is very familiar, but through a deeper examination of the story from the perspective of the men of Israel, God gives us a formula for how to eradicate the condition of men-who-pause. As black men, we must become more engaged and committed to the plight of our people. We can no longer remain satisfied with unsatisfactory conditions. No longer can we ignore what we see and know to be the truth about our troubles. As brothers, we must learn to stop, look, listen, and engage. If we fail to do this, then the fabric of the black race will forever remain unraveled at the seams, and the thread of the black male as a collective force will remain detached from the fabric of society.

As any doctor would do, I must tell you the prognosis concerning the symptoms of men-who-pause. You can manage this condition. You can beat it in the end. But, here are some tips for avoiding men-who-pause:

1. **Make sure your surrounding environment is not conducive to producing men-who-pause.** Just like the men of Israel, we must see what surrounds us, and at any hint of trepidation, we are not to compound our troubles with fear. We are to engage because when symptoms are attacked early, it can stop the spread of infection.

2. **Make sure you check your temperature.** Men-who-pause leads to arrested development, which causes frustration. David

became irate because, although Israel was the army of God, they allowed Goliath to taunt them and frustrate them so they would not engage. To alleviate the fever of fear, we must drink from the cup of living water and take the medicine of faith and hope.

3. **Make sure you check the time and the season.** Israel was in a season of war and a time of battle. We must be prepared when the men-who-pause season comes, and take preventive measures to combat the condition before it is too late. But even if infection sets in, God has designed a peak period after which men-who-pause loses its effect. The Bible says that Goliath taunted Israel for forty days, but after forty days, God sent David as an antibiotic to wipe out the bacteria.

4. **Make sure you take the right medication.** Saul wanted David to put on his armor in order to face Goliath, but Saul's remedy was not the right one to fight this kind of condition. All David needed were some smooth stones and a slingshot because this remedy had served him best before when he had faced enemies in the past. We need to use what God has given us to fight our fear.

5. **Make sure you consult with your doctor.** David talked with God and took his advice. He trusted the divine diagnosis and prescription for getting rid of the problem. When we talk to the Lord, we should recognize that the battle is not ours alone. It's also the Lord's.

6. **Make sure you know your prospects for survival.** David knew God would give him the victory over Goliath because David's survival meant victory for all of Israel. When we eradicate men-who-pause, that secures the survival of black people as a whole.

7. **Make sure you adhere to all preventive measures.** We need a healthy sense of perspective, and taking certain preventive measures can secure that perspective for us. As men, we have to incorporate a diet of diligence in helping our fellow brothers

and enlist and engage our brothers to fight against our fear of the unknown.

The fact is that David embodied the principles of a predestined Christ. David was not only a champion for Israel, but he established a legacy of greatness that had far-reaching implications into the future. David's determination lasted throughout the ages and yielded what we know as the manifestation of Jesus Christ, the son of David. I believe David's character as shown forth in his confrontation with Goliath is why God chose the lineage of David and the tribe of Judah to be born into. God sensed that the people within the makeup of David's family carried a great determination not to be held back by fear.

I am so glad that Jesus did not allow the crucible of the cross to deter him from his destiny. I believe that one thing that enabled Jesus to endure was that he understood that on the other side of his cross lay waiting for him a crown of glory! That same understanding should encourage and sustain us.

As I think about what Jesus has done and continues to do for us, I am reminded of how our forbears came through the devastation of the Middle Passage only to pick up the mantle of determination on the other side of the world in the Americas. It is through the blood, sweat, and tears of their efforts that we are now afforded the opportunity to reach our full potential.

Brothers, inside of us is the Spirit of God, coupled with the blood of our ancestors. We were not born to succumb to the condition of men-who-pause, but we were born to supercede any condition that impedes our progress! Brothers, we are survivors, so live life well and prosper in the Lord!

chapter four

when black men LEARN
how to BEAT the blues

Joe S. Ratliff

Why art thou cast down, O my soul? and why art thou dis-
quieted in me? hope thou in God: for I shall yet praise him
for the help of his countenance. (Psalm 42:5)

allow me to begin by saying that our society has
created an environment where black men are constantly facing
the blues in their lives. Whether we are watching television,
reading the newspaper, listening to the radio, or simply talking
to people in passing, black men are always being attacked, as if
we are people who have been cursed by God. We are placed
into categories that are never favorable; we are portrayed as
thieves, treated like animals, and forever seen as inferior to other races. I think it is also important that we understand that
these views are not new to our generation. For decades, black
men have consistently been treated as "less than"—less than
human and less than adequate.

To justify their power and control, the plantation masters said
that black men were savage and hypersexual. To strengthen racial
control, late-nineteenth- and early-twentieth-century scientists
and academics concocted pseudoscientific theories that said black
men were criminal and mentally defective. To justify lynching
and political domination, the politicians and business leaders of
the Jim Crow era said that black men were rapists and brutes. To
roll back civil rights and slash social programs, Ronald Reagan,
Rush Limbaugh, and Pat Buchanan said that black men were

derelicts and lazy. To secure big Hollywood contracts and media stardom, some filmmakers say that the "boyz n the hood" are gangbangers, drive-by-shooters, dope dealers, and car jackers. To hustle mega record deals and concert bookings, some rappers and comedians say black men are "niggers" and "bitches." To nail down book contracts and TV talk show appearances, some black feminists say black men are sexist exploiters or, simply put, "dogs."[1] The reality is that no matter where we look, black men are seen as a threat to society. But thanks be to God that, regardless of how society portrays black men, because we were created by God we can find assurance in his Word to give us strength in the midst of our crisis!

In Psalm 42, we find words that were written by the great King David. The book of Psalms is filled with wonderful liturgy from the Old Testament, beautiful lyrics that always uplift and encourage and words that will inspire humanity to grow closer to the Lord. The psalms have become so effective and have made such an impact upon this world that even nonbelievers can quote the famous Psalm 23. It is clear that God's hand was on David as he wrote words that would change lives for centuries to come.

Allow me to say that David was not writing simply in theory, but David was writing because he knew what it is to be down with the blues. David was not only someone who had been down, but he was also someone who had been lifted up by the King of kings! That's great news to black men in our world. It assures us that God has the power to transcend human thoughts and motives, and that he has the power to lift us to levels that others will have to respect!

In this passage, David began with a crescendo of praise and adoration, and then resigned himself to the fact that his soul was full of longing and forever being drained of its strength. In fact, it appears as if, in spite of all of his successes, David was now a man who, in contemporary words, had the blues! Life has a way of allowing us to have good days, successful experiences, life-changing encounters, and joy that seems endless. However, the simple truth is that, no matter how great we are, just like David, we will experience some days when we feel as if we are suffering from the blues.

Therefore, I just want to take this time to speak to black men and let them know what the Bible says about beating the blues. I will use Scripture to help us with a principle that serves as the acronym BLUES. I believe this scriptural acronym can help us, as men of faith, to lose the blues and find the joy that God wants us to have. Allow me to give five Scripture references that will help us beat the blues and assist us through this mysterion called life.

believe the positive

As African American Christian men, we can beat the blues if we *Believe the positive*. Philippians 4:8 says, "Finally, brethren, whatsoever things are true, whatsoever things are honest, whatsoever things are just, whatsoever things are pure, whatsoever things are lovely, whatsoever things are of good report; if there be any virtue, and if there be any praise, think on these things." If you want to experience deliverance from the blues, you have to change your thinking in order to change your life. One of the reasons many of us as black men cannot achieve our dreams is simply because we have allowed society to condition us to see limitation as inevitable. Brothers, if you are ever going to achieve greatness, you have to know first that you are great—not because of your abilities, skills, finances, connections, education, or status in life, but simply because you are a child of God!

Psychologists would say that if you feel down and at a low point in your life, you are suffering from clinical depression. Sociologists would say that you are lonely, isolated, and alienated. Educators would say that you are unmotivated and disengaged.

However, as a Christian, you have to be able to know that you are simply going through something that God will ultimately bring you out of. If you are going to make it, you have to be able to see the positive in everything you do.

I remember one Sunday someone said to me, "Pastor Ratliff, you travel so much you need to have your own plane." After pondering the comment, I responded in a positive way by saying, "I do have my own plane, but every time I get on, two hundred other people board with me." Having a positive mind will free you from your past burdens, pains, and dilemmas. That is why Paul says, "Whatsoever things are of good report, think on these." My brothers, you have to decide for yourself in life that, regardless of what comes your way, you will not remain a victim, but you will always strive to become a victor. You ought to shout, not because of what you are facing but because you know that, in the end, you will have the victory!

I read a story that inspired me; it was about a man who was watching a football game while in Hawaii. Because of the time difference between the continental U.S. and the islands, the NFL Monday Night Football game occurs around midafternoon in Hawaii, but the local TV station delays its telecast until 6:30 in the evening. When the man's team played, he was too excited to wait for the television broadcast, so he listened to the game on the radio, which broadcast it live. He also watched the game on television later that evening. Since he knew his team had won the game, that knowledge influenced how he watched it on television. When his team fumbled the ball or threw an interception, it was not a problem. Although he thought it was bad, he wasn't upset because he knew that, regardless of how the game was going, in the end, his team was going to win the game.[2] Brothers, you have to know that God has already given us the victory as black men through salvation, and in the end, we will win the game and receive eternal life if we keep our faith in him!

look for purpose

Second, we must *Look for purpose*. We find encouraging words in 1 Peter 5:10, which tells us that after we have suffered for a while, God will establish us, strengthen us, and settle us. If you are living in this world, God has a purpose for your existence. Socrates once said that a life that has not been examined is a life that is not worth living. In order for us to beat the blues, we must seek God and ask God for his purpose in our existence. Regardless of our many accomplishments in life, if we are outside of the will of God, we are not operating in his purpose for us.

My brothers, purpose is when you know that you are called to a task and there is nothing that can extinguish your fire. When you understand your purpose in life, you are able to pray, "Father, whoever or whatever is in my life that you have not placed, please remove, and whoever or whatever is not in my life that you desire, please place." This is a prayer that releases all control in your life and allows you to focus on the will of God. As men whom God has called to lead, we must be able to follow his commands and directions if we are going to become effective in our communities, homes, and churches.

As a young lad growing up in Lumberton, North Carolina, I never understood what waiting on your purpose meant. It sounded crazy to me until I matured in my faith. I learned through various experiences, good and bad, that God's hand was in control and that there was a purpose for everything that I was going through. It's comforting to know that whatever you are going through is only because God has allowed it to take place. I am certain many of us have raised questions such as, Why am I going through this? I am innocent, so why am I in prison? Why didn't I get accepted to the college of my choice? Why didn't I get called by that church to be the pastor? How long will these storms last? Will my marriage ever turn for the better? Will God ever forgive me? We have to understand that since God is in total control, he knows his purpose for our existence and whatever he allows to happen is designed to get us to his purpose.

use the promises of god

Third, we must *Use the promises of God.* As Christian men, we all have promises that God has given us. Unlike human beings, God will never forsake his promises. However, the dilemma that many of us face is that we do not know how to accept the promises God has made! As a consequence, we spend much time focusing on our problems instead of on God, who is our problem solver. Romans 15:4 teaches us that, through patience and the comfort of Scriptures, we have hope. Once I realized the power of God's promise, I never found myself in a state of doubt because I knew that, although I may have a little trouble, there are some things that God has promised me. Perhaps the reason many of us find it difficult to trust the biblical promises of God is because we reduce God to the promises of human beings, and since people have failed us, we deduce that God's promises will, likewise, possibly not be fulfilled.

When I was growing up, my grandfather, whom I loved dearly, was someone who never let me down. He was my best friend, my solid rock, my anchor, and my incarnation of stability. He supported me with finances while I was attending Morehouse. He always offered hope in desperate situations. I don't care how many times I messed up or what the circumstance was, he always ended his dialogues with me by assuring me that everything was going to be all right.

Now, I don't know about you, but when we live in a world where we are constantly torn down and berated, it is always good to have someone who is able to let you know that all will be well. However, when my grandfather passed from earth to eternity, everything around me was shaky. It was at that precise moment in my life that God allowed me to focus on a particular Scripture:

Philippians 4:19. I read it several times, and through the Holy Spirit, God taught me that although my earthly provider had departed, "I, the Lord, your eternal provider, will supply all of your needs according to my riches in glory if you simply learn how to focus on the promises that I gave you in my Word." Not only did God teach me to trust him, but he also gave me the power to be patient. I learned that, in life, if you are not in a hurry, you always have time. Too often in life, we expect God to move in our time, not realizing and accepting the reality that God's timing is always better than our time because he knows what he has destined for our lives.

My brothers, learn how to count on God's promises! But just in case you cannot remember some of his promises, allow me to share some with you: "For the LORD your God is he that goeth with you to fight for you against your enemies, to save you" (Deuteronomy 20:4). "Wait on the LORD: be of good courage, and he shall strengthen thine heart: wait, I say, on the LORD" (Psalm 27:14). "God is our refuge and strength, a very present help in trouble" (Psalm 46:1). "Seek ye first the kingdom of God, and his righteousness; and all these things shall be added unto you" (Matthew 6:33). "Whosoever believeth in him should not perish, but have everlasting life" (John 3:16). "God hath not given us the spirit of fear; but of power, and of love, and of a sound mind" (2 Timothy 1:7). Brothers, quit complaining. God has given us everything we need to make it. The only thing we have to do is rely on his promises, wait on the Lord, and know that he will see us through!

encourage other people

Fourth, we need to learn how to *Encourage other people.* The reason many men are falling by the side of life today is because when we are down, we are not willing to help one another up. Our male egos have had a negative impact on society. As men, we should seize every opportunity to give encouragement to one another.

Brothers, encouragement is oxygen to the soul! Our days are dark enough to bump into the dangerous walls of life. One of the highest ideals in life is the duty of encouragement. It is easy to laugh at men's ideals; it's easy to pour cold water on their enthusiasm; it's easy to discourage others. The world is full of discouragers. However, as Christian men, we have a duty to encourage one another.

Many times, a word of praise or encouragement has kept a man on his feet. However, the sad reality is that most men don't want to help other men, and as a consequence, we have no strong support. It is a sad dilemma today that, in most churches, the hardest ministries to develop are ministries that need men! When we look in our society today, records reveal that in 1999 there were 757,000 black men in federal, state, and local prisons. There were only 604,200 African American men enrolled in higher education. These numbers are revealing—in 1999 there were 25 percent more black men in prison in the United States than in college![3]

How many of the bothers in prison are your cousins, fathers, friends, uncles, brothers, and even some pastors you may know? Brothers, unless we learn how to help lift one another up in our society, homes, communities, and churches, we will never reach and fulfill the promises of God! Second Corinthians 1:4 teaches us that we must help one another whenever we are in trouble. The text does not name specific troubles; it just says, whenever someone is in trouble, we need to help that person. The Greek says "help them in *any* trouble."

Brothers, learn how to encourage one another, regardless of the trouble. If you have a brother who was locked up and is having a hard time to get back on his feet, encourage him. If you have a brother who has made some serious mistakes, don't knock him further down in life; encourage him. If someone's marriage is shaky, don't remind him of what he has done wrong; lead him to the Word of God and encourage him. Whatever you do, learn how to encourage people along the way. And just in case you get selective memory, always remember that before you were where you are—before you became the minister, before you received that promotion, before you were named senior pastor, before you started reading the Bible, before your marriage was reflective of God's purpose—someone had to help you along the way and give you words of encouragement! Part of the secret of beating your own blues is encouraging another to get through his.

sing god's praises

Finally, after you have *Believe the positive, Look for purpose, Use the promise of God,* and *Encourage other people,* you must *Sing God's praises.* Praise is the authentic expression of your gratitude through your attitude for the altitude to which God has carried you. I know I have a reader who can testify that when you are experiencing the blues, if you learn how to sing God's praises, you can make it through! Psalm 66:2 says, "Sing forth the honour of his name: make his praise glorious." One of the reasons we cannot make it through our blues is because we fail to give God the praise while we are experiencing the blues! Praising God is the key to our deliverance. Praising God brings hope to a hopeless situation. Praising God lifts you out of despair. The psalmist was so convinced about the power of praise that he said, "I will bless the LORD at all times: his praise shall continually be in my mouth" (Psalm 34:1).

Not only is it recorded in Scriptures, but it is also written in the pages of black history. Our enslaved ancestors were beaten while pregnant, dragged through the streets, knocked down to the ground, laughed at, ridiculed, and dehumanized, but they did not allow their temporary circumstances to steal their eternal hope. They were so committed to praising God that they sang, "Before I'd be a slave, I'd be buried in my grave And go home to my Lord And be saved."[4] They kept on thinking about the power of God and said in their minds, hearts, souls, and spirits, "We may be down, we may be slaves, it may seem as if we are in a hopeless battle, but we will overcome some day."

Brothers, when you get in the blues, sing praises to God! Come into his church with praises on your lips and thanksgiving in your heart. And I promise you, when men start praising God, homes will be renewed. When men start praising God, marriages will be renewed. When men start praising God, prison doors will be opened. When men start praising God, foundations will be laid. When men start praising God, lives will be changed!

My brothers in Christ, when you praise God, joy will come. And the joy that you have—please know that the world didn't give it and the world can't take it away. When you praise God, regardless of what you are going through, you can say like the psalmist, "Weeping may endure for a night, but joy cometh in the morning" (Psalm 30:5). And if someone should ask you how you can praise God in the midst of your blues, simply respond by telling them, "Praise is what I do and praise is who I am!!"

Believe the positive, Look for purpose, Use the promises of God, Encourage other people, and *Sing God's praises.* That's how black men can beat the blues.

NOTES

1. *Earl Ofari Hutchison.* The Assassination of the Black Male Image. *(New York: Touch Stone Publishing, 1994).*

2. *Edward K. Rowell.* Fresh Illustrations for Preaching & Teaching from Leadership Journal. *(Grand Rapids, Mich.: Baker Books Publishing, 1997).*

3. *Bill Maxwell: "Grim Statistics for African-American Men,"* St. Petersburg Times *online, Jan. 4, 2004.*

4. *"Before I'd Be a Slave (O Freedom)." Words by William E. Barton, 1899. Negro spiritual in the public domain.*

chapter five

hands full of HONEY[1]

Lance Watson

[Samson] came to the vineyards of Timnath: and, behold, a
young lion roared against him. And the Spirit of the Lord
came mightily upon him, and he rent him as he would have
rent a kid, and he had nothing in his hand: ... And after a
time he returned ... and, behold, there was a swarm of bees
and honey in the carcass of the lion. And he took thereof in
his hands, and went on eating.... (Judges 14:5-6,8-9)

samson is one of the most enigmatic and strangest
characters in the entire Bible. Filled with power and yet fractured
by faults; packed with possibility and yet sapped by sin—he is a
solemn reminder to all of us that promise, power, and potential
alone are not enough to make life worthwhile, to make a person
truly successful, or to make a ministry effective. Black men, you
can be extremely gifted, terribly talented, profoundly powerful,
and especially anointed—but all those benefits combined are not
enough to deliver a person determined to go astray. For example,
Steve Howe was voted Rookie Pitcher of the Year in 1980 after
a dynamic season with the Los Angeles Dodgers. He was herald-
ed as the next Nolan Ryan and admired for his talent. His fast-
ball was consistently clocked at more than ninety miles per hour.
His team was renowned for producing Hall of Famers, but Steve
Howe's potential evaporated when his struggle with cocaine
became public. The Dodgers had to release him, and even after
repeated chances at recovery and redemption, he still could not
strike out his habit or retire his addiction.

Samson, too, had the potential to be in God's Hall of Fame. His life was teeming with potential and promise, but his urges and issues short-circuited his potential, sabotaged his promise, and diverted his power. As you will see, my brothers, his story is a cautionary tale of tremendous power wasted in trivial pursuits.

As God's anointed adjudicator, Samson could have been one of the greatest leaders in the complete chronicle of sacred text, but he threw it all away. And it behooves all of us, as black men, to examine our own hearts and habits, to check our own predispositions and propensities, lest we too miss the mark and neglect our golden opportunity! Samson reminds us that no matter who you are, what you have, or where you are, if you don't keep yourself in check, your potential can be squandered, your promise can be lost, and your power can be neutralized.

That is the basis of the contemplative life—it is the art of self-evaluation, for just as Samson had both internal and external enemies to meet and master, so do you and I. The thirteenth chapter of Judges opens with the woefully familiar phrase, "And the children of Israel did evil again in the sight of the LORD." The people of Israel picked the perilous path of disobedience to God, again and again. Their history is littered with repeated disobedience. Time and again, they deserted and disappointed God, and yet, each time the flow of blessings tapered off and the stack of troubles began to mount, they would cry out to God for healing and help—and God would deliver them.

The Israelites' external enemies were the Philistines—Greeks who had been forced out of their homeland near the Aegean Sea and who conversely had established a beachhead on the shores of Southern Palestine. The Philistines had erected five cities (known as the Pentapolis) on the coastal plain and possessed a monopoly on the manufacturing and smelting of iron, and they did not permit any competition. Because of that, they possessed a strategic stranglehold on the economic and military activities of the nation of Israel.

Yet, because God is God and because God is good, God will never leave those who trust in God without hope. Therefore, the Lord raised up a group of men and women who served as judges to act as human vehicles of divine deliverance. Brothers, we must believe that God always has somebody to do his work, pursue his will, and fulfill his plan! And if we take no other assurance from our walk of faith, black men, I hope that each of us would become possessed by the reassurance that we belong to God.

We're not serving by ourselves. We're not preaching on our own. We're God's sons and God's servants. No matter what they say about us—as men, as fathers, as husbands, as employees, as students—no matter how they treat or mistreat us, we belong to God! Just as God raised up judges for them, so God sent Christ for us to save us, secure us, sustain us, and sanctify us so that we might become the people of God, experience the grace of God, walk in the power of God, and do the work of God.

Our text is Judges 14:1-10, which relates the tale of a young, unarmed Samson in the strength and vigor of his youth, wrestling with and defeating a lion that surprised him on the road. This serves as a metaphoric reminder for us that Jesus Christ has slain the lion of our gravest fears, deepest anxieties, and worst ills. On the cross of Calvary, Christ triumphed over death, hell, and the grave, and set us free from bondage, that we might experience the glorious liberty of the children of God.

every life has its struggles

This stirring story about Samson teaches us is that every life has its struggles. Your struggles may not be mine and mine may not be yours, but every life has its struggles, no matter what our title, position, popularity, or possessions. There are still tears to shed, crosses to carry, burdens to bear, struggles to endure, and mid-night floors to pace.

As servants of God, we do have a joyful journey, yet I know you will agree that the way is not easy. We struggle with family, finances, fights, and frustration. We struggle with betrayal, brokenness, and bitterness. We struggle with people who promise, but don't deliver; with people who gossip, but don't give; and with people who smile in our faces, while all the time desiring to take our places. Brothers, people will challenge us because they don't understand us. However, we as black men must remember, sometimes the way is hard, the road is rough, the going is tough, and the hills are hard to climb. Brothers, we must accept the reality that there are mountains to face, valleys to scale, and rivers to cross. No servant of God goes through this world untried, untested, and unchallenged. We don't and won't glide through life or slide into our destiny on beds of ease or cars of comfort.

Every life has its struggles. Often struggles start early, struggles are stressful, and struggles can be startling. While every life will have some serious struggle and definite difficulty, with the power and peace of the Lord, we can do more than take it; we can also make it, regardless of what comes our way.

struggles start early

Judges 13:24-25 tells us that when Samson was a child, he was filled and empowered with the Spirit of God. You don't have to be elderly to be elected, nor ancient to be anointed. God's Spirit moved in the boy Samson and began to prepare him as a youth to become the one man that God could and would use to stand against the enemies of the people of God.

It is because of what he would be *then* that the enemy faced him down *now*. Brothers, you may not know who you are, but the enemy does. You may not sense your potential, but the enemy does. You may not know exactly how the Lord desires to use you, but the enemy does. You don't have to be afraid of the enemy, because the enemy is afraid of you!

The reason that people are lying on you now, jealous of you now, conspiring against you now, hating on you now is because of your *then*. Whenever God releases power into a person, the enemy has to get started early to try to abort that anointing, pollute that promise, and pervert that power, because he knows that if you ever become what God has appointed and anointed you to be, you will be a force to be reckoned with!

The enemy is not concerned with who you are *right now*; his issue is with what you're *about to become*. He's not fearful of what you possess in this moment, but he is fearful of what you shall have in the future. He knows that you now possess a dream, but soon you will have a plan. He knows that you now possess a desire, but soon you will have a strategy. He knows that you now have an itch to do, but soon you will have a craving to be. He knows that if you ever get an authentic glimpse of what you really are or are going to become in the eyes of God—some things are going to change in your life, my brother!

God develops us effectively so that he can use us impressively. Every life and every ministry has its struggles, and they start early. We struggle to get started; we struggle to manage the multiple obligations and expectations placed upon us; we struggle to be relevant; we struggle to have a meaningful ministry to people who are drowning in an avalanche of information; we struggle with those who are treading water in a culture of outplacing and replacing, of deployment and unemployment, and of beeper bondage and cell-phone captivity. We struggle because we know that the future is ours, by design or default, and that no matter how hard we try, we cannot hold the future to a frozen version of the past. We struggle to claim this cultural moment and bridge the gap between doo wop, be bop, and hip hop.

Brothers, many of our struggles start early because this is the time when we lack maturity. This is the time when we have yet to learn the deceptive tools of the enemy. This is the time when we haven't been exposed to many of the games of life. This is the time when we are most vulnerable.

That is why the contemplative life is so critical. A contemplative life is a life of prayer. A contemplative life is a life of discernment where you understand that it's better to stand for something than to fall for everything. Such a life is one in which everything that shines is not silver, all that glitters is not gold, all good-byes don't mean you're gone, and everybody smiling in your face is not your friend.

struggles are stressful

Being a black male in this society can be stressful. We are expected to perform and produce as a leader in our homes and communities, but we aren't always given the chance to prove our talents and display our skills. It is stressful to have expectations placed on us but opportunities taken from us. It is stressful to attempt to be a real man in the eyes of your family but are unable to address their basic needs. It is stressful to participate in this society as a contributor when you are viewed as a taker and not as a giver. Your life is lived in a metaphoric fishbowl where every word, deed, and move is open to observation and scrutiny. It's stressful.

As a servant of God, men, we need to be ready for difficult days. Jesus said in John 16:33, "In the world you shall have tribulation: but be of good cheer; I have overcome the world." Stressful struggles will come.

Sometimes, the struggles are internal. Samson was a Nazirite, consecrated from birth to the service of the Lord, raised under the pressure of parental expectation that he achieve great things (Judges 13:2-5). Yet, everything seemed to go awry when Samson developed an overwhelming attraction for Philistine women.

And Samson … told his father and his mother, … I have seen a woman in Timnath of the daughters of the Philistines: now therefore get her for me to wife. Then his father and his mother said unto him, Is there never a woman among the daughters of thy brethren, or among all my people, that thou goest to take a wife of the uncircumcised Philistines? And Samson said unto his father, Get her for me; for she pleaseth me well. (Judges 14:1-3)

You can almost imagine the stress-filled, late-night conversations of Mr. and Mrs. Manoah, saying in their bewilderment, "Why is God allowing this to happen? Why is this boy so headstrong? Didn't God promise us a deliverer, so how did we get this delinquent?" But verse 4 tells us that it's what they *didn't know, couldn't see,* and *did not comprehend* that made all the difference: "But his father and his mother knew not that it was of the LORD, that he sought an occasion against the Philistines: for at that time the Philistines had dominion over Israel." God was working in Samson's life—despite his bad choices. God moves in a mysterious way, his wonders to perform!

God does not need to manipulate or mechanize us like puppets. Through our choices, both good and bad, God works out the divine purpose for our lives. That's why no matter what people say to you or about you, no matter how many times you've fallen down, no matter how long you've been wrong, know this: God can still use you!

The *bend* in the road is not the *end* of the road, my brothers, unless you miss the curve! God chooses and uses whomever God wants to, however God wants to. We keep trying to package and dispense God—to put God in a neat little box of religious approval where, based on our definition of moral maturity, theological accuracy, denominational polity, charismatic suitability, and doctrinal particularity, we get to say who's in and who's out, who's approved and who's not. But God will not be boxed in. God can use anybody, anytime, anywhere to do anything that God wants to!

The community is crumbling, schools are failing, prescription drugs are expensive, substandard housing is prevalent, racial profiling is commonplace, and politicians are stressing. On top of this,

Johnny can't read, Mary can't write, cousin's on dope, parents are without hope, and friends can't cope. Everybody has some struggle, and struggles are stressful. Yet, even our struggles are designed by God to strengthen us.

That's the reason the Canaanites were in the Promised Land. God had promised the land to the Israelites, and yet they still had to face and fight the Canaanites, Midianites, and the Amalekites who were living in the land. God permitted the struggle so that the Israelites would appreciate the land once they got it, so that they would learn to lean on God, look to God, and depend on God. God knew that the struggle would make them strong. Struggles start early and struggles are stressful.

struggles can be startling

Struggles come when we least expect them. Have you ever been caught off guard where some stuff happened that you weren't looking for? Perhaps I know that I should have expected it, but I didn't. I expected welcome; I got worrisome. I expected support; I got struggle. I expected faith; I got fear. I expected evangelism; I got excuses. I expected praise; I got problems.

In the text, you will notice that Samson was alone much of the time. He was alone when he first saw Delilah; he was alone when he killed the lion; and he was alone when he returned and found the honey in the lion's carcass. His experience is true to the life that you and I experience. If we would follow Jesus, we have to make our peace with loneliness. In many of our struggles, loneliness will be our only companion.

Here and there we find a friend, but in order to make it, you have to manage lonely days and lonesome nights. Sometimes, it will be just you and Jesus! Samson was alone when the lion attacked, and also notice that he was empty-handed. The Scripture says Samson had nothing in his hand (v. 6). He didn't have a sword, spear, or javelin; he stood there unarmed, unprotected, and unequipped. And yet he had to face and fight a lion who startled and struck at him along the way.

Sometimes we feel unarmed and ill equipped. Sometimes we think, "I don't have the tools, the talent, the connections, or the strength to fight this fight." But this text reminds us that, like Samson, our strength flows from a secret source. Samson's strength was not in his biceps, his protruding pectorals, or even in his Nazirite hair. His strength was in the Spirit of God, and so it is with us. No matter how good the preacher or how effective the servant, in the end, we are just like a kite. It may be well constructed, perfectly manufactured, ornate, and expensive, but if the wind doesn't blow, it's of no use.

Our strength comes from God! Without God, nothing is possible, but with God, even the impossible is possible. I don't know what you think or how you feel or what you believe, but I know that I need God. I cannot make it without God!

It's the Spirit of God working in us that empowers us to stand. Never forget that. Even when you are empty-handed and alone, brothers, *you still have the Lord!* I may not have friends, but I have Jesus. I may not have resources, but I have Jesus. I may not have support, but I have Jesus, and as long as I have King Jesus, I don't need anybody else! "I can do all things through Christ which strengtheneth me" (Philippians 4:13). "If God be for us, who can be against us?" (Romans 8:31). My brothers, trouble will come, but trouble will also pass. Every life has struggles, yes, but the Spirit of God gives us strength to survive our struggles.

every life has its sweets

There is one more thing to remember—every life has its sweets.

Look again at the text in Judges 14. Sometime later, Samson came across the dead carcass of that former foe, and he found that a tribe of bees had established a hive—an impromptu manufacturing facility—inside it. Samson paused and in grateful abandon took a handful of honey before continuing his journey. Thank God, we are not always wrestling lions; sometimes, we get to eat honey! We fall down, but we get up. We struggle, but we succeed. We may weep during the night, but we do have joy in the morning. We have heartaches, but we also have hallelujahs.

We serve a God who regularly makes our life sweet. Every day we are given health and strength. Every day there is food on our table. Every day gets sweeter than the day before. No wonder the songwriter wrote, "'Tis so sweet to trust in Jesus, and to take him at his word; just to rest upon his promise, and to know, 'Thus saith the Lord.'"[2]

Thank God for the sweet moments! Thank God for making a way out of no way. Thank God for making your enemies leave you alone. Thank God for healing your body. Thank God for building you a bridge over your troubled waters. Thank God for meeting you in the courtroom. Thank God for putting food on your table. Thank God for lifting up your bowed-down head. Thank God for wiping your tears away. Thank God for precious memories. Thank God for sweet moments.

We face lions, but we also eat honey. Every life has its struggles, but every life has its sweets. You just have to know where to find them, how to claim them, and what to do with them once you have them in hand.

find sweets in a place of previous struggle

This text teaches us that *sweets are often found in the place of previous struggles.* Samson found honey in the carcass of the lion he had defeated. When he looked at the lion's dead body lying by the side of the road, he could say without fear of contradiction, "I survived you! You were stronger than me, but I survived you. You startled me, but I survived you. You struck me and stressed me, but I survived you." Every now and then, you have to permit yourself to walk down memory lane and recall the struggles you've already survived, my brothers. Remember the trouble you came through, the heartaches you walked through, and the haters who tried to kill you. Look over your shoulder—*and give God some praise.*

You thought you had me, but I survived you. You were sure I'd fall in that trap, but I survived you. You lied to me and on me, but I survived you. Never forget the struggles you have come through. No matter how high you rise, remember where you came from. Remember that you took the stairs, not the elevator. You came through something to get where you are. That's some sweet stuff! Your story brings God glory.

Brothers, no matter what is going on in your life, you are not now what you used to be. Back then, you used to be broke, busted, and disgusted, could barely be trusted. Back then, you used to be under stress and in duress. Back then, you used to be down so low that down was looking down on you—but God brought you out. What you came through ... you shouldn't be here! I should have been dead. I almost let go. My feet almost slipped. I almost lost my mind up in here, but now God has made my life sweet. Things that used to depress me now bless me. Things that I thought would break me can no longer shake me. Back then, my life was bitter, but now God has made my life sweet.

claim sweets by scooping them

Second, by studying this text, I have discovered that *sweets have to be scooped.* The honey was there, but it had to be scooped out. God will never do for black men what we have the power, intelligence, and ability to do for ourselves. The honey is there— get to scooping! Whatever you want in your life and for your family, you've got to scoop it out.

Preach it; then practice it. Teach it; then try it. Mouth it; then model it. Talk it; then walk it. Say it; then show it. You can do great things, achieve great heights, walk in great places—but you've got to scoop it out. You can be more prayerful, careful, powerful, and faithful, but you've got to scoop it out. You can be more effective, efficient, excited, and enthusiastic, but you've got to scoop it out. You can build a wider network, live under a greater anointing, walk in power and talk of victory, but you've got to scoop it out.

Now I realize that this can be problematic, because we live in a cultural moment where everybody feels that life, God, the government, and everybody else owes them something. But, you've never seen a bird standing in a worm line, waiting for the third of the month and talking about "Chirp-chirp, I'm waiting for my worm." Why? Because a bird understands intuitively and instinctively that, if I'm going to eat, I have to get up before sun up, get on my branch, and when something moves, go get it. You've got to scoop it out.

Brothers, go back to your community and get to scooping. Go back to your church and get to scooping. Go back to the point of your pain—there's some honey there!—and get to scooping.

Notice that God put the honey in a place that could only *accommodate it temporarily.* The carcass was decaying, while Samson was enjoying. All of our honey is stored temporarily. That's why you can't be married to your method or tied to your tradition. What works today won't work tomorrow. You cannot play CDs on an 8-track player. The music is the same, but the method has to change!

The honey was stored in a temporary container and the underlying message is *don't get stuck in your sweet spot.* Enjoy it, but don't expect sugar-coated situations to last forever.

sweets are for sharing

I have also discovered that *sweets should be shared with others.* Samson shared the honey with his parents. When God blesses you, you need to share it with somebody else. Since God has blessed you, you ought to share it. You need to know that you can live without worry, fight without surrender, pray without conceding, shout without shame, work without discouragement, hope without disappointment, believe without delusion, suffer without despair, wait without anxiety, work without compulsion. You can think more clearly, feel more deeply, speak more truthfully, love more extravagantly, risk more boldly, serve more creatively, give more lavishly, and live more abundantly.

You remember that we talked about how Samson's struggle with the lion was a metaphoric reminder of Jesus, who has conquered every one of our lions. We mentioned how, on the cross at Calvary, Jesus overcame the deadliest lion of all—death. He shares that victory over struggles with us. But, victory isn't the only thing Jesus shares. Now he offers to us a handful of honey! He offers us the honey of salvation, liberation, inspiration, exaltation, determination, and motivation, so that we can live our dreams, work our plans, scale great heights, and do great things. The risen Christ has honey in his hands, and he's inviting us to take a taste. "O taste and see that the LORD is good!" (Psalm 34:8).

Black men, you need to know today that Christ has risen! You need to know today that you serve a risen Savior! You need to know today that he is a living God! I know he lives, because he walks with me and talks to me. I know he lives, because I feel his presence and experience his power. I know he lives, because he turns my dark clouds into bright skies. I know he lives, because he dries my weary eyes and raises my spirit. I know he lives, because he has proven to be my all in all. I know he lives, because every time my foes and my enemies tried to attack me they stumbled and they fell. Every life has struggles, but because of Jesus, my hands are full of honey.

NOTES

1. *"Hands Full of Honey" originally appeared in the Summer 2004 issue of* The African American Pulpit. *It is printed here, in a modified version, with permission of Hope for Life International, Inc., Publisher of* The African American Pulpit.

2. *"'Tis So Sweet to Trust in Jesus." Words by Louisa M. R. Stead, 1882. Public domain.*

section two

TRUMPET SOUNDS to address
the INTERPERSONAL ILLS of our day

chapter six

on being a BLACK FATHER
in america

J. Alfred Smith Sr.

And Joseph knew his brothers, but they knew him not.
(Genesis 42:8)

in his seminal book, *invisible man,* ralph ellison
said that the black man in America is (as the title suggests) invisible.[1] While people see us physically, they do not see us psychologically. They discount our presence and the value of our lives. While people see black men, they wish they did not. And if, by chance, they do see or recognize our presence, they see our shortcomings rather than our strengths.

How true are Ellison's words and his description of black life in white America. The ideas of Ellison ring true today, even though they were stated decades ago! Since 1619, when the black male first came to America as a slave, to the present year of 2004, the black man remains a slave to white economic interests, and he is as invisible now as the white man's brother as he was then.

It is a sad reality that white America remembers Willie Horton, but forgets Frederick Douglass. White America does not mind it if we hustle for pennies, as long as we do not reach for greatness. And as great as Tiger Woods is, white males who fear his ability to outshine them tell Tiger not to serve fried chicken on our golf courses. White America forgets about Joe Louis, Jackie Robinson, Satchell Paige, and Magic Johnson, but remembers O. J. Simpson. Let us not forget that the "Admiral of the Spurs," David Robinson, built a school.

Last year, Pete Wilson, anchorman of Channel 7 here in Oakland, interviewed me in the Family Life Center. He toured our campus and visited parolees learning computer literacy in our skills center. He proceeded to describe, on television, the ugly stories about black-on-black crime. In contrast, Wilson has done no special TV features on the Enron scandal. None of the white men in Enron, who stole the pensions of hundreds of workers, have been held up as "white-on-America" criminals. The thieves, guilty of insider trading on Wall Street, are not portrayed as examples of white-on-white crime. We black men are rendered invisible not because our oppressors are blind; instead, we are rendered invisible because too many of them are myopic—they are shortsighted or nearsighted.

The predicament of the black male in America is much like the predicament of Joseph in the Old Testament. Misunderstood by his family because he was a dreamer and sold into slavery by his brothers, Joseph lived in a strange country far away from home. My African American brothers, how many of you feel estranged, far from home?

Although given favor in Potiphar's house, Joseph was wrongly accused by Potiphar's wife and thrown into prison. Later, he was put in charge of all the prisoners—but forgotten by the chief butler. Like some black men today (such as Hurricane Jackson), Joseph served two years in prison for a crime that he didn't commit. Brothers, how many of you feel imprisoned, feel convicted of a crime that you did not commit, such as "driving while black"?

But that was not the end. Joseph interpreted Pharaoh's dream and became high up in Egyptian government (rather like Colin Powell has done today in America). Joseph married an African woman and became the father of African children. He didn't forget God, as seen by how Joseph named his sons: Manasseh (meaning, "God made me forget all my toil and my father's house") and Ephraim (meaning, "God has made me fruitful in the land of my affliction"). Joseph blessed his blood relatives who named him.

Then Joseph's father died. Joseph's guilty brothers, much like white America, reasoned that Joseph would seek revenge. Joseph's response was: "Fear not: for I am in the place of God? But as for you, ye thought evil against me; but God meant it unto good" (Genesis 50:19-20).

But history did not improve the conditions for Joseph's descendents. Exodus 1:6 says, "And Joseph died, and all his brethren, and all that generation." Verse 8 goes on to say, "Now there arose up a new king over Egypt, which knew not Joseph." Joseph's descendents became invisible in Egypt. In the same way, in our modern Egypt, the pharaoh of white America sees us but does not see us. This is what Ralph Ellison was referring to.

Brother, have you noticed that we are seen as tokens—visible in war, visible as entertainers, and visible as sports figures? But we are invisible in boardrooms, invisible where policy is made. We are visible as consumers, but invisible as producers. Brothers, so many of us are visible as welfare recipients, but invisible as millionaires. We are visible as mack-daddy, jive-talking pimps, and we are visible as foul-talking, womanizing rappers. We are visible as academic failures and street-smart killers who invented and continue to perpetrate drive-by shootings. But, we are invisible as good husbands and fathers and inspired leaders in the church. We are invisible as Ivy League graduates and conscientious politicians and activists who devise fair legislation and healing community services to remedy the ills in our communities. We are invisible as ethical and creative businessmen. We are invisible as passionate participants at local YMCAs and other youth facilities where we serve as tutors and mentors.

Brothers, you've seen the statistics. Some 792,000 black males are warehoused in prisons—more than those who live in all of San Francisco, the twelfth largest city in America! But we are invisible as leaders and scholars such as Michael Eric Dyson, Henry Louis "Skip" Gates, Freddie Haynes, Jawanza Kunjufu, Gardner Taylor, Cornel West, and Jeremiah Wright. These leaders remind us that there are ways to be visible in this world that seeks to make us invisible. They show us that we can be both heard and seen. They encourage us to speak up, to sit at the table of power. They encourage America to remove the lens that distorts its vision and renders us invisible.

Admittedly, we live in a racist world where we are judged by the color of our skin and not by the content of our character. How will we, as black men, respond to the invisibility that is imposed upon us? How can we make ourselves visible? And when visible, what image will we portray?

Will we show that we can rise in spite of our crippling, externally-imposed liabilities? We *shall* rise because God, according to his riches, will strengthen our inner selves. With God's mighty power, we shall defeat our inner demons and our outer demons. These invisible demons, like cancer, eat away at our confidence, eat away at our morals. These inner demons drive us to destroy each other. These inner demons, like magnets, draw us away from our wives and our children. These inner demons defeat us with AIDS, alcohol, and drugs.

Brothers, we cannot get lost in this invisibility syndrome, whatever its source. Why? Because God has sent Jesus to reach and rescue us from these demons. The Bible reminds us that Jesus will redeem us. Jesus will restore us! Jesus will reconcile fathers to their wives and children. Jesus will redeem us. Jesus is in the business of spiritual ecology!

So, black men, there is hope! We know this from the Bible. We know this from our collective and individual experiences with God. We know this from our rich legacy. We know this from our intimate encounters with the Lord of lords and King of kings. We know this because of God's track record of days gone by. While we are invisible to some, still we rise. We are the last hired and the first fired, but still we rise. While we are talked about in degrading ways, still we rise.

We may be invisible and unrecognized in the eyes of some of our earthly brothers and sisters, but in the eyes of the God who created us and formed us, we are visible. We know that we are visible, because we know that our heavenly Father keeps his eyes not only on the sparrows but also on all of his children.

Society may try to paint a colorless canvass that excludes us as principle players on the global landscape. The mass media may attempt to portray an image of us as irresponsible men and as a menace to society. But God will serve down justice like a mighty wind and establish his Nubian population as men of honor and as men of valor.

Like Joseph, we may very well be rejected by some people. However, the good news is, we are already selected by God. God knows that we are consistent fathers. He knows that we are caring fathers. He knows that we are capable fathers. He knows that we are compassionate fathers. He knows that we are courageous fathers. He knows that we are Christian fathers. And the reason that God knows is because he made us in his own image.

Brothers, keep striving to be your best. Brothers, keep striving to do his will. Brothers, keep striving to walk in his power. Black men, always remember that God will always have you on his cosmic radar. Black men, always remember that you will never be invisible to God!

NOTE

1.   *Ralph Ellison,* Invisible Man. *Random House, 1952, p. 3.*

"Rejected but selected"

chapter seven

somebody WAKE UP daddy!

Rodney Maiden

And these words, which I command thee this day, shall be in thine heart: And thou shalt teach them diligently unto thy children, and shalt talk of them when thou sittest in thine house, and when thou walkest by the way, and when thou liest down, and when thou risest up. And thou shalt bind them for a sign upon thine hand, and they shall be as frontlets between thine eyes. And thou shalt write them upon the posts of thy house, and on thy gates. (Deuteronomy 6:6-9)

a few years ago, toy developers were advertising a new board game called "Don't Wake Daddy." The primary objective of this game is to see who can get to the refrigerator without waking up Daddy. If you get up at midnight with the munchies and you need to raid the refrigerator, you better not wake up Daddy. While on this mission, you go through different obstacles, such as, "Don't step on the cat" or "Don't step on the squeaky boards or stairs." When you land on a certain space, you have to push a little lever beside the bedpost and see if Daddy will wake up. You hold your breathe when you push the button on Daddy's alarm clock three times. You don't know if he'll wake up or not, but the object of the game is "Don't wake Daddy." If you wake up Daddy, you lose the game.

I believe that we *need* to wake up Daddy today because we are losing our families, friends, and communities. Brothers, I believe the world and society in which we live is playing this game, because we see signs and evidence all around us that too many daddies are sleeping. We see a deterioration in our society, a decline in our families, and all of the problems in our homes and communities let us know that somebody, on purpose, refuses—or fears—or doesn't know how—to wake up Daddy! With this in mind, I want to talk about "Somebody Wake Up Daddy!"

Daddies, it is essential that you know one thing: The only legacy you will ever truly leave behind is the children you have brought into this world! Now, you're going to leave a legacy in your children whether you like it or not; you are going to leave a legacy whether you believe it or not. Whether you want to or not, you are going to leave a legacy.

It might be a legacy of abuse. It could be a legacy of mess. It could be a legacy of chaos. It could be a legacy of promiscuity. It could be a legacy of abandonment. It could be a legacy of anger. On the other hand, it might be a legacy of peace and compassion. It could be a legacy of love and patience. It could be a legacy of hard work and steadfast determination. It could be a legacy of being a family man. It could be a legacy of all kinds of things, but you're going to leave a legacy. The Bible makes this clear!

Fathers, we've been napping for too long. It's time for somebody to wake up Daddy! Why? Because the way we ought to serve our families is the same way that Christ serves the church. And Christ serves the church in three ways: as prophet, as priest, and as king. As a prophet, the father speaks from God to his children. As a priest, the father speaks to God for his children. And as a king, he governs and qualifies himself to lead his children by his willingness to serve. So, Daddies, we are called to be prophets! We are called to be priests, and we are called to be kings of our families!

Sadly, because so many of our brothers have nodded off to sleep, we are experiencing a sharp decay in our society, particularly in the African American community. Because fathers are not in their prophetic position, they aren't carrying out their responsibilities within the family. Somebody, wake up Daddy!

In the book of Deuteronomy, in chapter 6, God instructs the fathers. It's the father's responsibility to train and teach his children diligently. Where do you teach them? God said, "You teach them at home." God said, "When you sit down at the table, you instruct and you give guidance." Father, teach your children what it means to love God with all of their heart, with all of their mind, and with all of their soul! Teach them by precepts and example. They must follow you. They must see the positive, godly, Christian example that you set. They must see you as a role model.

Daddies, God told fathers to teach without ceasing, morning, noon, and night (v. 7). This is a spiritual imperative. The Lord said, "Even write it on the door post, on the gates." So you must realize that, even when your children leave home, they leave with your training. They leave with your instructions. They leave with your teaching. They leave with your examples. They leave with your legacy. Even when they come back, they run into Daddy's teachings. They run into Daddy's instructions. They run into Daddy's guidance. How can this be? Because Daddy takes what God has taught him and teaches it to his children, over and over again. In addition to meeting our children's basic needs for food, water, shelter, and safety, every day, we must supply them with the right guidance, the right instructions, the right training, and the right modeling.

Many of the problems we're having today are in direct correlation to the spiritual sleeping of too many daddies. Somebody ought to wake up Daddy! Somebody *must* wake up Daddy! Brothers, wake up from your nap of despair. Brothers, wake up from your nap of pain. Brothers, wake up from your nap of self-doubt and self-hatred. Brothers, wake up from your nap of complacency. Brothers, wake up from the lies that have been taught to you about your God.

Fathers, yes, you ought to be esteemed. You ought to be respected stewards who are greatly rewarded. But, there's a problem in fatherhood today that is a direct result of the crisis in manhood. We seem to be in a spectrum ranging from being a fabulous father to a dead-beat dad. America's transition from being a producer to a consumer nation has brought a marked change in our mindset of "family," which has led, in part, to our present-day problems.

Young people without the teaching and nurturing and admonition of the Lord from their fathers begin to desire to be satisfied themselves rather than working to satisfy others. This attitude has helped to bring on this "me" generation, where the goal is to satisfy me, myself, and I. Each person's goal is to satisfy self, a purpose that degenerates into the present theology of deifying the self. Because of the absence of fathers in the home and the absence of our teaching, instruction, and guidance, our children's values are not what they ought to be. And this self-aggrandizing philosophy, together with negative media representation of African Americans fathers, does not help!

Fathers, you watch TV the same as most people do. You see that the media portrays fatherhood as something that can be easily discarded, as a big joke. Everything is talking and mocking against fathers as the head of the home. Other profound influences have produced results that are staggering today—rap music seems to be outselling gospel music; romance books seem to be outselling spiritual books, and so on. The reason there is a moral and ethical decline in our communities today is because fathers are asleep. Like Rip Van Winkle, Daddy is asleep and missing.

And, brothers, we must understand that, although a lot of single mothers are saying, "I'm both Momma and Daddy," we as black men must be the first to stand and speak within our prophetic designation and gentle disposition and inform them that they cannot be both. Because God did not design her or equip her to be both Momma and Daddy. So, Daddy is just not there. And when you try to play both roles, you're playing a role that God did not give you.

Growing children are often left to themselves, with just the television to raise them. Now, more African Americans have computers and the Internet and Xbox and PlayStation 2, etc. These things are robbing our children of their time and their mind; they are stealing their initiative and killing our relationships with them. Studies indicate that for every seven hours spent watching television, children spend one hour reading. Most children spend more time watching TV than they do studying, leaving little time for positive and spiritual role models.

Sadly, black children watch an average of six hours of TV per day, twice as much as white children. After attending school for six hours, watching TV for another six hours, and sleeping for eight hours, how much of the remaining four hours is spent on studying? How much is spent listening to the radio? How much time is left talking with their parents? How much time is spent reading the Bible? Too many black children are not doing well in school. One major reason for low student test scores is due to poor stewardship of our children's time. No wonder our teens are in trouble!

Where else should these values be instilled, if not in our own homes? Somebody, wake up Daddy! Government never raised a child and never will! Nothing more powerful determines a child's behavior than his or her internal compass—her beliefs, his morals, her sense of right and wrong. The character of a society is determined this way, by means of individual morality that accrues social capital from generation to generation. Fathers, what cultural inheritance are we leaving our children?

Many of our young people are growing up in a fatherless society, growing up without someone who is responsible for giving them the nurture, the teaching, and the training that God has entrusted to the fathers. Hence, not only are our children today growing up without fathers; they are also growing up without morals, without a moral compass to guide their thoughts, decisions, and actions. For those who don't find their worth by immoral, illicit, or illegal means, suicide becomes a viable option. Suicide is the second leading cause of death among American youth today. Somebody wake up Daddy!

Those who survived their teenage years find themselves caught in the backwash of this baby boom society whose culture and attitude still dominate the American discourse. And this new baby generation, ranging in age from 18–29, seems almost to be rebelling against rebellion. Apathy and alienation have given way to disengagement. Why? Because too many of our African American children don't have positive role models. They don't have positive people to look to in the home or community. The absence of fathers in the home to give them direction leaves many of our children "spiritually homeless." Somebody needs to wake up Daddy!

The greatest mission for men, and especially for us fathers, is not only to correct what is wrong in adults, but to reach out and teach what is right with our children and youth. Where values and goals are not taught in the home and where educational processes deny responsibility for moral values, where will young men and young women find such precepts? The Bible says it's to be taught in the home.

Father, we must not be deceived into thinking that the institutions of philosophy and the adulterated authority figures or media-made role models would, could, or should teach our children the principles upon which to build their lives. The home is the place where these values ought to, and *must*, be instilled into their lives. And it's the father's responsibility to do this! The problem that we're having is that too many fathers are neglecting that responsibility—our spiritual obligation to our children! Fathers are sleeping on the job, taking some sort of long hibernation or vacation from their responsibilities. Somebody wake up Daddy!

For those without a father or a fatherly role model in your life, you ought to get guidance from a friend. Get guidance from a neighbor. Get guidance from a church leader. Get guidance from somebody who loves the Lord! Getting a fatherly role model is important because young men must be mentored in the ways of morality, in the ways of goodness and righteousness. And men, God is going to hold us responsible. God is going to hold us accountable! Statistics are clear: We have more young African American men in prison than we have in college; we have more African American men in special education than we have in gifted education; we have more African American men living in poverty than in wealth.

A few years ago, I had the opportunity to visit Grafton prison. It was heart breaking. We walked through those gates with our visitors' badges on and went through a strict security system. As we went from cell block to cell block, it broke my heart to witness a sea of young African American males locked up—men who got caught up in the system, men who didn't have anyone in their lives to guide them properly.

I sat down and talked to those young men, because I just wanted to know how many of them grew up with a father in the home. Not one of them could say, "I grew up and I had a good father in the home." Some said, "I grew up with an abusive father." "I grew up not knowing who my father was." "I grew up and somebody told me that a man down the street was my daddy, but he never came down the street to see about me." No guidance. No instruction. No training. No love. No sense of belonging. So, they learned it from the street. They learned survival from the guys on the corner.

How many men believe that it is our responsibility, as fathers, to teach our children as the Bible says in Deuteronomy 6? Need more convincing? Look at Ephesians 6:4, which exhorts, "And ye, fathers, provoke not your children to wrath: but bring them up in the nurture and admonition of the Lord." How much longer will we sleep, preferring not to understand or accept the reality that it is our duty, our obligation, and that God is holding us responsible?

We have a priceless resource in African American men, many of them older men, who have found the answer to the world's problems through Christ. Those godly black men need to focus our efforts on mentoring our youth. Men, we cannot allow the wisdom, the experience, and the knowledge to die with us! We must invest the spiritual, physical, and material resources that God has entrusted to us and make every effort to incorporate them into the lives of our young people. Somebody ought to wake up Daddy!

And teen fathers need to know what real fatherhood is all about. They need to understand that, if you're big enough to make a baby, you ought to be big enough to take care of one. Being a man is not determined by how many women you can score with, or by how many babies you can produce. Fido can do that! It's no big deal how many girls you can have on the side. Being a man is a function of whether you can stay with one—and treat her right. That's what manhood is all about. And our sons are not going to find this out, they're not going to learn this, except from men like you and me who are right now in the church. They can only have real role models in men who claim to know Jesus, in men who claim to know Christ as their Lord and personal Savior.

Daddies, God is holding us responsible to teach them. *Family.* What thoughts or visions come to mind when you hear that six-letter word? *Family.* What comes to mind when you hear that very powerful word? The Greek word for family *(patria)* means "father's house." Do you not know, men, that you are a human representation of God the Father himself?

Our children are growing up with the misconception of who and what God is because they have no appropriate example in the home. They think God is an abuser. Why? Because you are an abuser. They think God is a deserter. Why? Because you are a deserter. They think God is unfaithful to his church. Why? Because you are unfaithful to your wife or your children's mother. And the only concept of God that they have is you! What image do you want to portray of our Father God in heaven?

The only way we can show our children what God is like is by being godly men! We do this by taking on God's characteristics and attributes—not by imposing our failings on him. When our children look at us, when our children hear us, when our children walk with us, and when our children watch us, they will be able to place a vivid picture in their mind of what God the Father is like.

Brothers, you are expected to model within the family that which you know to be true of God. Brothers, you know that God is a provider. Brothers, you know that God is a healer. Brothers, you know that God is a comforter. Brothers, you know that God is always there for you, when times are rough. Well, that is what our children expect and deserve from us. Brothers, if you are sleeping, you can't provide for your children. Somebody, please wake up Daddy.

If we are doing what God has called us to do, our children would know that God is just. They would know he is loving, he is caring, he is true to his word, and he is a provider. How? Because we are faithful, we are just, we are loving, we are caring, we are true to our word, and we are good providers!

Fathers, our problems are sown as seeds in the life of our children and reaped when they become adults. That's why it's imperative—it's important, it's high time, it's crucial—today, right now, immediately—that somebody wake up Daddy! "And that, knowing the time, that now it is high time to awake out of sleep: for now is our salvation nearer than when we believed" (Romans 13:11). If Daddy ever wakes up, then all that is wrong would change in our home, in our community, in our churches, and in our nation.

What type of legacy are we leaving our children? What spiritual inheritance are we bequeathing to our children? And what spiritual legacy and inheritance are we going to leave our children? Let us pray that we become to our children the type of father that God is to us.

chapter eight

thugs, pretty boys,
and the JESUS STRATEGY

Frank A. Thomas

And He [Jesus] said to them, "Why did you seek Me? Did
you not know that I must be about My Father's business?"
(Luke 2:49, NKJV)

the key phrase that we want to pay attention to
in this text is "my Father's business." From the age of twelve, Jesus
was clear that he was about God's business. It is an unfortunate
reality that, while Jesus was clear about his task, many times we
as black men are *not* clear about the Father's business. We think
we clear are about another business—the business of women, the
business of making money, the business of sports, or the business
of sex with women. Sex is imbedded deeply in the psyche of most
men, and because sex is imbedded so deeply, many men are about
the business of women more commonly by default.

The gift of sex that God intended for good has become distorted. Regrettably, around the world, in every culture, sex is often
viewed as nothing more than a service or favor that women grant
or bestow upon men; therefore, men have to compete to have sexual access to women. Further, it appears that such intimacy is a
more risky enterprise for women than men; therefore, women
generally are more sexually reticent than men. Women know that
the risks of sex are large, including pregnancy, childbirth, sexually
transmitted diseases (STDs), and AIDS. If men are to procreate
and women are more reticent about sex, then men have to compete with other men for the reproductive future of women.

thug strategy

In order to compete with other men, men develop several strategies. The first strategy is violence, or what I call the Thug Strategy. Violence, "thuggery," is one of the ways that men compete with other men for sexual access to women. Violence deals with the competition by eradicating it, and that often takes three particular forms: (1) murder gets rid of other men with whom you would otherwise have to compete for women; (2) physical or emotional abuse takes women "off the market"—either by making them afraid to go into the market for a better deal or by taking them off the market altogether by killing them; and (3) sexual violence, specifically, rape, allows men sexual access to a female that they would never have the ability to compete for.

The thug strategy is violent men perpetrating violence for the sake of soliciting, impressing, or controlling women, or with the intent of subduing or killing other men for access to women. A tremendous amount of male violence is connected to conflict over women. For example, Tupac Shakur and Biggie Smalls were friends. As I understand it, Tupac made some remarks that he "got with" Faith Evans, Biggie's girlfriend, and it was on between the two of them. The result is that both of them are dead, and neither murder has been solved. And Faith Evans has since moved on with her life.

My Brothers, think about it: two men are dead; the woman is alive. Men, women, and violence have functioned together since the beginning of human history. Thugs are men who perpetrate this violence against men and women alike—the hard-look, hard-life, hard-jail-time, kicking-butt and taking-names, gun-shot, drive-by, gangsters-of-the-neighborhood thugs. Thugs—crotch-grabbing and trick-playing thugs. Too pitiful to pay the cost, so through violence, they aim to be boss—thugs. Objectifying females, they don't care whose lives they derail—thugs!

Pretty Boy Strategy

The second way men compete for access to women is what I call the Pretty Boy Strategy. This strategy attempts to appeals to women through traits that women value. Women like certain kinds of men, and if you've got what women are looking for, you are "in the house." A few years ago, after the movie *How Stella Got Her Groove Back* came out, young Jamaican brothers were "in." Before that, the in-look was to be light skinned with "pretty" eyes and "good" hair. The mantra of the pretty boy is "Aint nobody dope as me, I'm just so fresh and so clean and smooth." Women like men who have the clean look. Pretty boys—stylin'-and-profil-in', laid-back-just-like-the-Mack, clean-clothes-and-not-a-hair-out-of-place—pretty boys. They are smooth, suave, sophisticated, romantic, ladies man—pretty boys. Women love pretty boys.

Pretty boys understand how to play on ladies' emotions. After all, who better to understand the dynamics of someone desiring to be pretty than someone who has the same desires? If the truth is to be told, pretty boys display a lot of feminine characteristics. Pretty boys, like many women, must have every hair on their head in place, must keep their nails manicured, must be dressed to kill, refuse to go outside when a pimple forms on their face and are constantly in search of affirmation.

In fact, part of the pretty boy strategy is to exclusively date pretty women for the sole purpose of fulfilling his need for psychological affirmation. All too often, he sees his mate as a reflection of himself or at least what he desires to be in the eyes of the public. His mindset is beauty complements beauty. His aim is to charm and compliment the sister so that she in turn can compliment him. His goal is to find a lady who could be his trophy and arm piece before the eyes of other men and women.

Pretty boys tend to use chivalry as a tool for manipulation and stimulation of his would-be victim. They tend not to be violent, but to be insecure and shallow of substance. His ultimate goal is to be the roundtable discussion between his women and their friends.

The danger of the pretty boy strategy is it will land you in trouble over time because sooner or later the pretty girl that you fell in love with with find another pretty boy to take your place and that tends to render one exposed and vulnerable. It's at this moment when the pretty boys become violent and unstable. However, this is also the opportunity for the brother to grow up and discover his inner, spiritual, masculine beauty.

jesus strategy

Lastly, there is the Jesus Strategy. The Jesus Strategy is not about getting women, but it is about getting, following, and adhering to a relationship with God! For Jesus, God's business was first, and from God's business flowed the rest of life, including relationships with women. When we, as brothers, are about God's business, we can and will live a life that reflects our belief in Matthew 6:33: "Seek first the kingdom of God and His righteousness, and all these things shall be added to you."

During the time of our scriptural text, adults were supposed to attend the three major feasts in Jerusalem: Passover, Pentecost, and Tabernacles. (For many, this was impossible, but an attempt was typically made to get to the Passover at least.) Families often traveled to Jerusalem in groups or clans, particularly when a boy in the family had reached puberty. With puberty, a Jewish boy becomes a "son of the covenant." *Bar mitzvah* is what it is called today. It was considered helpful for a younger boy to attend the Jerusalem festivals for a year or two before becoming a "son of the covenant," so that he would realize what his new relationship entailed and with whom he was in covenant.

That is probably why Jesus was in Jerusalem at the age of twelve. And, since families often traveled in larger groups, Jesus was probably often out of his parents' company, hanging around with cousins So-and-so. But, then Mary and Joseph ran into cousins So-and-so and learned that Jesus was not with them after all. Only after a full day of travel had they missed him, and on the next day, they began their search for him.

Three days later, they found him. When they found him, Jesus was putting questions to the temple teachers—not boyish questions, but insightful and penetrating questions, such that might be asked in academies and places of higher learning. Jesus also gave answers to the questions he asked. Everyone listening was amazed.

But, his mother let him have it, child prodigy or not! Mary lambasted him; she chewed him out: "We have been looking for you, boy." Jesus responded, "Why? Why were you searching for me? Didn't you know I had to be about my Father's business?"

My brothers, I ask you, What is the Father's business? What is the Father's business for men? I do not think that the Father's business is the thug strategy, or Jesus would have been a thug. I do not think the Father's business is the pretty boy strategy, or Jesus would have been a pretty boy. The Father's business is the business of building a relationship with God and allowing that relationship with God to grow you into a "son of the covenant"—a real man! Jesus was after a purposeful and primary relationship with God. Jesus wanted to get his relationship with God established, and out of that relationship, he could be the kind of man with whom God would be pleased.

What kind of man is God pleased with? God is pleased with a responsible man. God is pleased with a dedicated man. God is pleased with a faithful man. God is pleased with a devotional man. God is pleased with a compassionate man.

We, as black Men, can and will please God a lot more when we are more about his business than our own selfish and self-centered business. God's business is to build a family and not destroy a family. God's business is to restore communities and not tear them down. God's business is to reconcile broken relationships and not foster havoc between one another. God's business is to get people to look at their potential and not suffocate one another's possibilities.

Brothers, a man's business is not about getting a woman; it is about building and maintaining a godly relationship with the women in our lives. It is not about making a baby; it is about making and taking care of a family. It is not about being violent toward our women; it is about nurturing our women. It is not about placing mental scars on the minds of our children; it is about providing an environment that will allow our children's minds to grow and be fed in a positive manner.

My brothers, sadly, in the present condition of the black family, seven out of ten babies born in hospitals do not have a father in the home. When a father is not present in the home, there are drastically increased odds that the child will grow up in poverty. When that black child grows up in poverty, it is difficult to compete with other races and ethnic groups, so we find ourselves in a permanent underclass. Because we are disproportionately in the permanent underclass, poverty becomes the curse of our existence.

I do not believe that God is honored by the behaviors and motives of thugs and pretty boys. Instead, I believe that men who want to be about their Father's business honor God! What does the father's business look like for men today? In other words, what is the kind of man with whom God is pleased?

First, it is the father's business to give a name and identity. Remember, in Jewish culture a child was not a legal person until some male stepped forward to give the child a name. Joseph stepped up and gave Jesus identity. Joseph was not Jesus' biological father, but Jesus would have been a nonperson until some male stepped forward to claim him and name him. That is God's business for black men: to claim and name. It is our business to claim and name our families. It is our business to claim and name our neighborhoods. It is the Father's business for men to give identity.

Joseph gave Jesus identity. A man who is concerned with the Father's business is about the business of claiming and naming.

Second, it is the father's business to teach a trade, a way to make a living. Producing a community that is economically viable—that is the father's business. Joseph gave Jesus a trade. Joseph taught Jesus a way to make a living so that Jesus was an economically viable member of society. Jesus was not on welfare. Jesus was not looking for a government handout. Jesus was not playing the dozens, playing the lottery, wheelin' and dealin', shuckin' and jivin', slippin' and slidin.' Jesus was not looking for government cheese or unemployment checks. Jesus had a trade. Jesus had a way to sustain himself and pay his own way, and teach others to have their own economic viability. Joseph, in taking care of the father's business, gave Jesus an example to watch and learn from, a role model. Jesus did not have to become or remain a carpenter just because his father had that trade as a profession, but Jesus did have to have someone show him how to work and how to earn a living for his family. That is the Father's business!

Third, it is the father's business to be a model of self-sacrificing service. That's why God sent Jesus. That is what Jesus was trying to explain to his family and the crowd—that he was on a mission from his Father. The father's business is to make sure that both his family and his community have a model of sacrifice and service. Jesus came to serve—to help others. Jesus came to feed the hungry, clothe the naked, and visit the sick. Jesus came to give rather than to receive. He came to help and not to hinder. He came to share and not to take. He came to provide service and not to demand being served. He did not come to get rich; he came to give all he had. He did not come to be a thug or to be a pretty boy; he came to be a servant.

And so, Jesus climbed that old rugged hill called Calvary because of service! It was for service that he let them hang him high and stretch him wide. It was for service that he hung his head and died. But, because he was about the Father's business, death could not keep him and hell could not hinder him, and God brought him up out of that grave with all power in his hands. If you are about the Father's business, poverty cannot defeat you. If you are about the Father's business, racism, unemployment, cancer, illness, or disease cannot stop you. If you are about the Father's business, God will raise you up!

Men, I have learned that, if you take care of the Father's business, then God will take care of your business. I didn't have the strategy of the brothers on the corner, but I was about the Father's business. So, without violence, without profiling, God gave me the woman I needed, a family to lead, and a spirit to serve. And, perhaps most importantly, God gave me my identity! My name is not Thug. My name is not Pretty Boy. My name is Son of the Covenant!

chapter nine

SAVING our BLACK BOYS in america

Jim Holley

And one of the multitude answered and said, Master, I have brought unto thee my son, which hath a dumb spirit; And wheresoever he taketh him, he teareth him: and he foameth, and gnasheth with his teeth, and pineth away: and I spake to thy disciples that they should cast him out; and they could not.... And he asked his father, How long is it ago since this came unto him? And he said, Of a child. And ofttimes it hath cast him into the fire, and into the waters, to destroy him: but if thou canst do any thing, have compassion on us, and help us. Jesus said unto him, If thou canst believe, all things are possible to him that believeth. (Mark 9:17,21-23)

there are considerable problems facing our family, community, and nation. One really doesn't know where to begin to address the multitude of circumstances and misfortunes within our collective lives. On a daily basis, our community faces a wide array of problems—poor housing, inadequate school systems, crime, violence, drugs, lack of health care, unemployment, underemployment, and family disengagement. Although I am concerned about all the aforementioned conditions, there is one issue that cuts to the core of my heart that I would like to discuss in this message. That issue is the disadvantaged status of our young black males.

Many organizations and civic groups are quick to render their perspectives on how and what to do about the crisis of our young black boys here in America. The Muslims say the solution is separation; the NAACP says it's voting power; the Urban League says it's educational programs; the government's answer to the crisis is to lock them up and throw away the key. Even many of our churches attempt to address the problem by constantly offering different kinds of programs.

I have come with a word that is from the stylus of a Gospel called Mark. I have a word, my brothers, that may cause you to be ill at ease with the practice of your religion as you have come to know it. I have a word that may cause some questions about the focus on your faith and the content of your commitment. I have a word that may make you squirm on the padded pews of your brand of comfortable Christianity. I have a word that may stop you in your tracks of "pseudo-piety" (as H. Beecher Hicks Jr. calls it), presumptuous religiosity, and self-indulgent spirituality—because when it comes down to saving all God's children, black males in particular, our religious lifestyles are inadequate and insufficient.

Unfortunately, many of our people have been characterized on a daily basis as valueless. In this country, millions of African American families live in poverty, yet this is the richest country in the world. If the church leadership and civil rights organizations have no real programs to save our boys, then who holds the agenda for them? For some reason, we are obsessed with talking about the problem, but are not doing what it takes to solve it. It troubles me that many African American leaders are able to articulate the social ills of our day, but only a few are able to step up and do something about them. Our churches and civic organizations must do a better job of dealing with our young black men.

Brothers, as you take a moment to think about the length of time that you have been in the church, how many relevant and life-changing programs have you participated in? You can count the years, decades, and scores of the revolving members, but you must admit, there has been a noticeable absence of black boys in the church. This is indicative of our failure to accommodate their unique needs! Somehow, somewhere, we have to interject the question, How can black boys be saved in America?

This is a ministry that we can no longer ignore. But before we can deal with their issues, we must first address our own. Brothers, we must deal with our issues and admit our faults so that the younger brothers can feel more comfortable expressing their hurts, pains, and concerns. This is a ministry that we can no longer leave up to some other culture or generation to address! It is time for us as black men to position ourselves to be available for the younger males. They are our children, our boys, and our responsibility.

We all have sons, nephews, brothers, and relationships to other boys in the neighborhood. We know that 70 percent of homes are without the presence of a father on a regular basis; 20 percent of the children live with another caregiver. And yet, we kiss the problem off. Where did we go wrong? How did we get this way? How did it end up like this? Is there any hope for these young, robust, intelligent, and talented young black boys—so many of whom, if projections are correct, will end up incarcerated, dead, on drugs, or disengaged from their families? Is there any hope for this future generation? Is there any hope for their becoming socially, economically, and educationally empowered? Again, I ask you, How can black boys be saved in America?

We have some soul searching to do in ourselves, our churches, and our homes. When I looked at this biblical text, I saw our black communities, our neighborhoods, our culture, and our dilemma—all under the microscope of scriptural scrutiny. You see, I'm not ready to give up on saving our young black boys! I don't want to accept the prognosis of the prognosticators. But, brothers, if we don't step up to the plate and do for our children the things that God has called us to do, then we can't blame the consequences on anyone else.

Brothers, if we don't take a stand, what does that say about the way we view our responsibility to serve our God, church, community, and families? Brothers, can we say that we have done our best to help our young black boys? Can we say that we have truly exhausted all of our resources to invest in their future? I've seen many attempts to teach and reach our younger brothers; some methods were successful and some methods failed. I have watched experts gather and debate, discuss, define, and conclude that they simply don't know how to save our black boys in America. May we see if we can get some answers to this question in our text?

Look at Mark 9:14, which says, "And when he came to the disciples, he saw a great multitude about them, and the scribes questioning them." The Bible records that there were several crowds: the dialogue crowd (the people), the symposium crowd (the teachers and experts in the law), and the workshop crowd (the disciples). And all of them are arguing, debating, discussing, and asking the same question that we are asking today: How can the boy be saved? While the experts are arguing, the boy is suffering. While the people are murmuring, the boy is being tormented. While the disciples are discussing, the boy's problem is going unsolved.

Isn't it the same for us today, here in America? While we are fighting over superficial, irrelevant things, our young black boys are suffering. While we argue over who is the better basketball player, our young black boys are suffering. While we are arguing with their mother, our young black boys are suffering. While we are debating whether or not the boy should go pro, the boy still can't read. While we are arguing, demonic forces are still saturating the spirits of our sons with evil thoughts. Brothers, we have done enough arguing, enough debating, enough discussing, and enough asking to last us three lifetimes. It is time for us to start doing, start praying, start believing, start investing, start inviting, start caring, start sharing, and start working on the solutions. It is our responsibility as black men to step up to the challenge. Simply put, it time for us to handle our business!

Then, there is the community, which puts distance between itself and the boy in order to ignore the problem. Black men, too many of us do the same thing today that the community did in the text. We brush this epidemic off as though it doesn't affect us directly. Well, it does. While we are arguing and pushing the issues of our youth onto someone else, the entire community is hurting. The father is hurting. The boy is hurting. And the community is hurting. The father can't enjoy his son. The boy can't enjoy his father. The community can't enjoy any unity.

Whenever the disciples of God—particularly the men—aren't in their rightful places and doing what God has called them to do, all the community suffers. Jesus expects us to be his disciples. As disciples, we are expected to assist Jesus by way of assisting others. It is when we serve the least of these that we are truly serving Jesus. But like in the text, all too often we are impotent—void of Jesus' power. The disciples couldn't save the boy then, and we are having problems saving the boys now.

Here is the father: bewildered, upset, disturbed, irritated, and agitated because the people whom he expects to be able to provide help aren't able to do anything. After all, the church had a reputation and résumé. What a powerful scene, and this is the picture of our community. This is a biopsy of living tissue in the early twenty-first century. This is the analysis of the status of our community! Meanwhile, the experts are arguing about "three strikes and you're out." The experts are arguing for a stronger crime bill. They argue that there should be less money for Head Start programs but more money for casinos. They argue that there should be less money allocated to fund after-school programming but more money to fund the building of more jails. They argue against improving the quality of our school system but argue for the privatization of our penal system. In effect, they say it is more economically feasible to incarcerate than it is to educate. They argue while our children are dying! And we, as saved brothers, allow it to happen. The question is still on the table: How to save the black boy in America?

In the text, the father has stepped up, but the "experts" only tell him what he already knows. "Your son has a demon." "He is ill." "He is dangerous to himself and others." "He is too unstable to stay at home and is disobedient in school." Some people have written him off as uneducable, unemployable, impossible, irresponsible, violent, dangerous, endangered, and he is branded "unsalvageable." Our boys are dying from self-destruction or benign neglect or both! How can black boys in America be saved?

There was a boy with a problem, and all the grown ups were arguing while the boy was suffering. Adults debate while our children suffer! Brothers, you and I must take some responsibility for changing the conditions of our communities. The world is not what it used to be, and yes, the church isn't what it used to be—or could be. One church says, "Use the rod"; another says, "No way." One says, "Discipline"; the other says, "No, no, now." We are having problems saving our boys because we are spending too much time arguing and debating when we should be about the business of loving and protecting.

There is a problem, and we have to identify the problem. Is there is a conspiracy as some claim? I believe that there is more than one conspirator. Long before Northerners invaded Europe, long before Christopher Columbus, long before the Mayflower, long before the Virginia settlement or Plymouth Rock, long before 1619, long before Crispus Atticus, long before Reconstruction, long before *Plessy v. Ferguson*, long before *Brown v. the Board of Education*—there was another conspirator, Satan. In the book of Job, while the sons of God were gathering, Satan showed up (see Job 1:6-12). You see, some preachers want to dismiss the devil, but if you are not careful, when you dismiss Satan, you may try to dismiss God next!

There are those who may be the instrument of a conspiracy, but the real conspirator is Satan. No human being or institution developed it; this is a satanic conspiracy. There is a devil because God said so! God asked the question, "What are you up to, Satan?" The enemy replied, "I am going to and fro in the earth, walking up and down in it" (Job 1:7)—and the New Testament tells us his intention: "seeking whom he may devour" (1 Peter 5:8).

When you look at this Scripture in Mark, there is a boy who was dominated by the devil. He was supervised, he was managed, he was lead, he was co-opted, and he was directed by the devil. The devil was his role model. The devil animated him, activated him, instigated him, and provoked him. The devil was his boss!

Any boy or man who would rather plan his funeral than his future has to be dominated by the devil. Any man who believes his addiction is more important than his children—that man is dominated by the devil. People who steal and rob for their drug habit are dominated by the devil. Any time a brother shoots another person over T-shirts, tennis shoes, sweaters, leather jackets, or another man's car, he is dominated by the devil. How can a father drive a Cadillac, while his children have no home? Why does any man, much less a young boy, commit rape? Why do our young boys keep their arguments in the streets rather than join debate teams in school? Why do our boys fight in the streets rather than wrestle and box in the gym? Why do our boys pack guns rather than books? I want to know, how can our black boys be saved?

In the text, the boy had a 'devil' problem! When the devil dominates our youth, he gives them a whole new ideology. Our children are being dominated by a mature manipulator and a master deceiver. And while everyone is still arguing, our black boys are suffering.

If our boys are going to be saved, fathers have to get involved. The last word from God in Malachi, before Christ was born, says, "And he shall turn the heart of the fathers to the children, and the heart of the children to their fathers, lest I come and smite the earth with a curse" (Malachi 4:6).

Fathers, you must escort your boys from childhood to adulthood! If you are not involved in your son's life, don't blame it on the school system. Don't blame it on the penal system. Don't blame it on the political system. Don't blame it on the economic system. It is time for us to share the blame. Blame it on the parental system—or the lack thereof!

All of us must find a black boy and take responsibility—and him—to Jesus! In this text, the father asked Jesus for pity on behalf of his son. To save our black boys, they may need pity, but they also need deliverance! They need salvation. They need healing. They need mercy. They need grace. They need direction. They need hope. They need self-esteem. They need internal fortitude. They need black men to show them the way to Jesus. They need black men to pray for them. They need black men to stand in the gap for them. They need black men to be a part of their lives. They need black men to reflect what men of God look like. So brothers, as you do all that you can for our young black boys, don't forget to take them to Jesus. Jesus can raise them up. Jesus can make a change. He can help us save our black boys!

God can make a difference in their lives. He healed the woman with the issue of blood, didn't he? He healed blind men and gave them sight, didn't he? He healed the lame and allowed them to walk, didn't he? He turned the water to wine, didn't he? God has the power. He is omnipresent. He is omnipotent. The best psychologist cannot compete with God. The best sociologist cannot compete with God. The best lawyer cannot compete with God. The best teacher cannot compete with God. The next time the question is presented, "How can black boys be saved in America?" you reply, *"By taking them to Jesus."*

chapter ten

kill them before they grow

Claybon Lea Jr.

Then Herod, when he saw that he was mocked of the wise men, was exceeding wroth, and sent forth, and slew all the children that were in Bethlehem, and in all the coasts thereof, from two years old and under, according to the time which he had diligently enquired of the wise men. Then was fulfilled that which was spoken by Jeremiah the prophet, saying, In Rama was there a voice heard, lamentation, and weeping, and great mourning, Rachel weeping for her children, and would not be comforted, because they are not. (Matthew 2:16-18)

there is a gentleman in Georgia who is a counselor at Savannah State University. He began his educational career as an educational therapist. Prior to obtaining his position at Savannah State, he was an emotional behavioral disorder teacher in the Georgia State Public School System for some five years. The gentleman is Michael Porter. Mr. Porter observed and was disturbed by a pervasive, unstated posture and practice in the Georgia School System perpetuated against African American boys. The posture and practice of which I speak is, and I quote, "kill them before they grow." That line became the title of Michael Porter's book, with the subtitle being *Misdiagnosis of African American Boys in American Classrooms.*[1] This book is one like Jawanza Kunjufu's *Countering the Conspiracy to Destroy Black Boys,*[2] a book that I cannot get out of my system. God has used it to give focus to this sermonic endeavor. Therefore, I preach on this occasion, making use of Michael Porter's book entitled, *Kill Them Before They Grow.*

Why such a strong title? For a sermon, that is very strong language: "Kill Them before They Grow." Why have I chosen such a strong title? Well, the answer is simple—because African American boys and their potential for future productivity are at stake. The title is strong because the potential, progression, and productivity of African American boys hang in the balance.

Several questions may come to the forefront of your mind in light of what I have shared so far. For instance, somebody may ask, "Who is being killed?" African American and Latino boys are being killed. "Well, who is perpetuating these atrocities?" Ultimately, Satan himself is responsible for the initiation and perpetuation of such a diabolical scheme. Penultimately, however, it seems that for many years, white male powerbrokers have set up an evil system that is sown into the very fiber and fabric of both this nation's history and its present condition.

Does that mean that all white males are prejudiced? Does that mean that all white males are responsible for this evil system that pervades our land? No, that is not what I am saying! No racial group has a monopoly on evil. For just as there are evil or bad white people, there are evil Hispanic people, there are bad black people, and there are also bad Asian people. However, when it comes to white males, there is a difference. Anyone who has ever lived in America and has studied "American history" knows that white males hold the greatest—though unearned!—power in this country, and they have used this power in questionable ways. Just think about slavery and the continuing discrimination in this great country referred to as the land of opportunity!

So, who is being killed? Black (and Latino) boys. Who is killing them? Satan, through white male powerbrokers. The next question is, "Where is this killing of our youngest black males occurring?" It is happening everywhere—namely, in the American educational, judicial, social, political, and economic systems. It happens as our young sons, brothers, nephews, and grandsons enter schools; for it is in school that they come to believe that they cannot achieve. Our young black boys are told that they talk too much, that they are too active, and that they ask too many questions. Too many of them are placed in special education programs or given drugs, such as Ritalin, under the guise of trying to keep them focused and on task. By the time many of our black boys leave elementary school, they have dropped out mentally and have lost their sense of pride and purpose.

There is significant revenue in such a posture and practice of killing black boys before they grow. You might wonder how a person can make any sort of profit from someone who ceases to be alive. Well, what you must understand, my brothers, is that there is more than one way to kill somebody! You can do it with weapons; you can do it with words; you can do it through war; you can do it through instilling worthlessness; you can do it through welfare; you can do it through a depleted workforce. There are all kinds of ways that you can achieve the same end. The most expedient way to kill someone—without a bullet or knife or physical weapon—is to take away that person's spirit, identity, vision, dreams, and purpose! Murders such as these take place using psychological weapons—another form or weapon of mass destruction! Yes, we are rightfully concerned about weapons of mass destruction in other countries and their potential to destroy America, but what about the psychological weapons that are manufactured in America and are being used to destroy the young black boys who are in their prime? Stereotypes, discrimination, racism, prejudice, and low expectations devastate black males everywhere—perhaps more than guns and drugs!

Brothers, I am sure that you have heard of a zombie. You know what a zombie is—the walking dead. A zombie is someone who is lost, mentally and emotionally. But zombies are valuable to some people. Zombies are worth something to the person or people who have placed them in that zombie-like state. Zombies can't think for themselves; they can't act for themselves; they are easily manipulated and controlled by the person who has made them a zombie. What does this mean for our young black males? How is this destructive practice carried out? It is carried out today in America in the same way that it was carried out in ancient Palestine, where Jesus was born.

I'm in the text now, because Jesus, in this second chapter of Matthew, had been born in Bethlehem. The magi, the wise men as we call them, had gotten word about this baby boy being born. They went to Jerusalem, which is where King Herod happened to be. And when they went there, they went acquiring about the king who had been born. Now what you have to understand is that Herod was the king. So, when they looking for a king that was just born, that said to Herod that he had better watch out because his throne was in jeopardy. So Herod told them, "Listen, brothers, I don't know where he is, but when you find him, why don't you just come on back through Jerusalem so I can go see him and worship him also?" Herod had no such thought in his mind; he wanted to find out in order that he might kill Jesus—before he grew. When the magi went and saw Jesus, on their way back an angel appeared to them and told them, "Don't go back the same way. Don't you go back to Herod. Go another way because God is at work in order that the prophecy might be fulfilled: 'Out of Egypt, I have called my son.'"

Remember, brothers, this destruction is sometimes done subliminally or covertly. Our sons do not see many positive images of themselves in textbooks and academic settings either. This is dangerous because our children spend thirteen years in school for 180 days a year. How many hours do they spend learning about their black heritage? How many hours do they spend learning about black males who are successful? Thirteen years is a lot of time to educate—or miseducate—a child as Carter G. Woodson lamented in his seminal book.[3] Thirteen years is a long time to instill dreams or to steal dreams! Thirteen years is a long time to assist in someone's growth or to assist someone's death.

We are all familiar with drive-by shootings and the destruction these acts wreak. But what about "drive-by teaching"? In such cases, teachers drive into schools, not to teach but to get a paycheck. Teachers who practice drive-by teaching spend little time in the black community; they spend little time in the homes of their students. Their black students are strangers to whom they have little allegiance, little commitment, or little sense of responsibility. When all is said and done, both drive-by shooting and drive-by teaching are deadly, in their own way.

It goes without saying that it is time to change the history books—all books—so that the American story reflects the African American story, the Hispanic American story, the Asian American story, the Jewish American story, the Polish American story, and so on. Our children are lost; many have no sense of history. We still have young people in the twenty-first century who only see a snapshot of Egypt in the history books. Few of them know that Egypt is a part of Africa. I think, my brothers, that you will agree—if you don't know where you come from, then you don't know where you can go. If you have no identity—no self-image—then any image will suffice!

In the biblical text, it says that when Herod learned he had been outwitted by the magi, he was furious. And with self-preservation in mind, he sent out the mandate to kill all of the Jewish boys under the age of two. He said, "Take them all out, if they are two years old and younger." Why select children two years of age and younger? Because it was believed that Jesus at that time could not have been more than two years old. Therefore, Herod issued this decree; he said, "Get the boys!"

It doesn't say anything about girls; if you have the boys, you have the seed. If you have the seed, you have the race and you have the people. We cannot reproduce without the seed that is found in our sons. If our black boys are killed before they grow old, then ultimately, the existence of African Americans ceases. Who benefits from the devastation, the destruction of the African American community? Who stands to gain from the loss of our black males? Think about it: Who stands to gain if racism persists? Who stands to lose if racism ends?

Brothers, we must talk to our sons, brothers, grandsons, and nephews! We must give our children their identity. We, as African American men, know what our children must have in order for them to reach their God-given potential. They need a strong black identity and they need it early! They need an identity that says, I am smart, I am kind, I am a good person, I am a good human being, I am a good son, I am made in God's image, I have a godly purpose ... I am a child of God!

They need an identity that will counteract the negative images portrayed of black males in books and in the media—on the news, in newspapers, on TV shows. They need an identity that will help them to understand that black males have as much potential as white males, as black females, and as any other group. Our black boys need to know that reading is their God-given right. Our black boys need to know that being smart is their God-given right. Our black boys need to know that being a gentleman is their God-given right. Our young African American males need to know that material possessions are superficial possessions, that hard work will be rewarded, and that no one can destroy their identity without their consent!

But there is more. Let's look at the controversial issue of Jesus' skin tone as a case in point. There are still some churches today that have pictures of a white Jesus. That is okay because Jesus can be whatever color, but on the other hand, it is something that we need to consider. Why? Because it says that the color of our Savior matches the color of our former oppressor. So think about it. If you are going to worship Jesus looking like that, then, you are still worshipping the oppressor. What this does subliminally is to instill a slave-like mentality. When the mind is in shackles, you are not free to think for yourself. Therefore, our children don't grow up seeing a picture of a Savior that looks like them.

Our young black boys need to know that God is not prejudiced! Brothers, I serve an unprejudiced Savior. I'm glad that God is not a racist. Jesus is my emancipator. Jesus is my liberator. Jesus is my rock. Jesus is my sword. Jesus is my shield.

Aren't you glad that, although Herod tried to kill him early, God said, "Not so!"? And you can be assured that, although the devil has tried to kill you early, God said, "Not so, not now, not ever!" Although we live in a society that profits from the psychological killing of our young men at an early age, we serve a God who will help our boys through all of the toils and snares that they may face. We serve a God who will never leave them nor forsake them. We serve a God who is still calling his sons out of modern Egypt. We serve a God who still produces wise men. We serve a God who still defeats the Herods of our day. We serve a God who still takes ownership of our lives. We serve a God who still echoes from the heavens above and says, "That's my child. I am going to protect him!"

I'm so glad that Abraham Lincoln is not responsible for my freedom. I'm so glad that the United States government is not responsible for my freedom. My savior's name is not Lincoln, but it is Lord. My emancipator's name is not Abraham, but it is Adonai. My emancipator, his name is Jesus! And it is through Jesus that we will find our freedom. It is through Jesus that we will fulfill our dreams. It is through Jesus that we will reach our potential. It is through Jesus that we will save our young sons, grandsons, brothers, and nephews. It is through Jesus that we will grow our young African American boys into strong African American men. It is through Jesus that we will be able to make it.

NOTES

1. *Michael Porter.* Kill Them Before They Grow: Misdiagnosis of African American Boys in American Classrooms. *Chicago: African American Images, 1998.*

2. *Jawanza Kunjufu.* Countering the Conspiracy to Destroy Black Boys. *Chicago: African American Images, 1997.*

3. *Carter G. Woodson.* The Mis-Education of the Negro. *Chicago: African American Images, 2000.*

section three

TRUMPET SOUNDS to address
the INTRA-PERSONAL ILLS of our day
(part one)

chapter eleven

DON'T count me out!

Rudolph McKissick Jr.

> And there were four leprous men at the entering in of the
> gate: and they said one to another, Why sit we here until we
> die? If we say, We will enter into the city, then the famine
> is in the city, and we shall die there: and if we sit still here,
> we die also. Now therefore come, and let us fall unto the
> host of the Syrians: if they save us alive, we shall live; and
> if they kill us, we shall but die. (2 Kings 7:3-4)

it has been said that there are many things that
you can live without, but the one thing you cannot make it without is *hope*. Hope is an attitude that can defy the odds when the
situation and even the facts are stacked against you. Hope is trusting in a power outside of yourself more than trusting in the power
of the situation. This four-letter word gives you a motive and a reason to keep living. In essence, hope can keep you alive when nothing else can. Hope can keep you alive when the prognosis is bleak.
Hope can keep you alive when the doctors say you are out of
remission. Hope can keep you alive when all signs say, "Give up."

Recently, when I was in Los Angeles, I saw on the news the story of a five-year-old little girl who had been found alive after having been missing along with her mother for ten days. When they
found the little girl, she was sitting next to the body of her dead
mother. Their car had gone over a ravine and landed in a wood-
ed area. After finding and talking to the girl, rescuers discovered
that the mother had lived for a day or so after the crash and was
constantly telling her daughter to keep hoping because somebody

was going to show up. The little girl said she just kept waiting on "the somebody" to show up. When reporters asked her who that somebody was, she responded, "The person Mommy told me was coming." She didn't know who Mommy was talking about, but just the fact that she was told somebody was going to show up was enough to keep her hoping! So, she said, she ate some noodles and drank some Gatorade that was in the car to keep her healthy until "somebody showed up."

As I recall this story, I feel like shouting! Life seems to have crashed for you and it looks like you ought to just crawl up and die, but hope is telling you that somebody's coming. All you need to do is stay in shape so that when they show up, you can get up. Hope can keep you alive when everything else begins to fall apart!

Now, I think I need to tell you that hope is different from making a wish. When you make a wish, you are looking for something that you know is not going to happen. Hope, on the other hand, is being certain that things will not stay as they are. Hope is being able to see beyond where you are and instead seeing where you are about to go. It is having a confident expectation. It's not about what God *might* do. It's not about what *might* happen. It's the conviction of expectancy in the face of contextual contradictions.

When you have hope, brothers, your condition or situation does not matter because you are not defined or confined by the facts of where you now find yourself. You are just foolish enough to believe—to know—that things are not going to stay like they are. I say "foolish" because, when you have hope, you can look like a fool to the people around you who are calculating your future based upon what they see as the reality of your present situation. But you know something they may not know—that whenever you calculate without God, it results in a miscalculation! That's why those who trust in God can always say, "No matter how dark it might look, don't count me out!"

That's what I see at work in this story in 2 Kings 7. Here, we find four men who suffered from the disease of leprosy. Their leprous situation should have had them resigning themselves to a life of misery. They have been put out of the city and forced to live on a colony with other persons who suffer from the same fate as they do. They have been forced to the outskirts of society. Society had set up rules and regulations for them because their worth was based on their condition. Nobody wanted to be around them. Nobody could touch them and they could not touch anybody. Everywhere they went, they had to announce their arrival by yelling with a loud voice, "Unclean, unclean!"

Can I take this argument a little further? Leprosy was a skin disease, which means that their problem was a problem that they could not hide. It was a situation that everybody could see. I mean, it's one thing when you can hide your issue! It's one thing when you can masquerade as if everything is all right because you can hide your situation. But how do you handle it when what you are going through is public domain? How do you handle when you're not known by your name, but you're known by your condition? How do you handle it when the definition of your destiny is determined by the description of your dysfunction? In the view of the ancient community, what those with leprosy had was more important than who they were!

There is some man right now who is in a position like those with leprosy. People know you by your problem, but they know nothing about you as a person. In fact, people have set limits for you based on a skin issue. It's a problem black men deal with everyday! We become statistically foreclosed on before we get started, because of our skin. Society has set rules that seek to govern our movements because of a skin issue. Our skin, by being different from the larger society, makes us deficient in the eyes and mind of many people. Our human-made skin problem has preassigned our value in society, and the enemy has just about convinced us that things will never change. Unfortunately, too many brothers have fallen into this sinister and misleading prognosis from other people.

Well, brothers, you need to read the end of the story! Look at verses 5 to 11. In the end, they were blessed, and it all happened because they refused to be counted out. They were able to receive all that God desired for them because they refused to be counted out. Can you imagine when they went to the gate to talk to the gatekeeper of the city? When you read the story in its entirety, you know that there was a famine in the land. So, the leaders put the leper colony outside of the city and left those folks there to die. Can you imagine the look on the face of the gatekeeper who left the lepers to die when he saw them blessed and healthy? He probably began to scratch his head in wonder and amazement. He was probably trying to figure out how they survived. I wish I could have given them a script, because the first thing I would have had them say to him was, "We know what you did, and we know what you thought, but don't count us out!"

Black man, you know some folk counted you out after the last trial you went through, but I know that I can find at least one witness who can testify today that when your enemy counts you out, that is when you can count on God to step in! Brothers, you need to tell everybody, "Don't count me out!" You must have your mind in shape so that you are able to think your way through the trials of despair and doom. You have to get tired of the enemy telling you where you can and cannot go, what you can and cannot do, who you can and cannot be. Rise up! Quit throwing your pity party. Quit acting like the tail instead of the head. You ought to tell somebody, "You can stay here if you want to, but I am about to rise up!"

Now, these four men were still lepers. God did not change their condition, but he changed their status. When you live life more abundantly, you can still have conditions, but you have to get a new status. God is looking for men who are willing to rise up and move up without having to change who they are. God can bless you being who you are! All you have to do is make the decision to rise up rather than stay down. Brothers, you have to make it up in your mind to be *counted* and not *discounted*. You have to press forward with a determination to be counted in this society and not counted out because of your skin. You must insist on being counted because of your skin and because of your rightful place on this world as a child of God.

Some of us feel that we are nobody and nothing unless we are surrounded by people. Brothers, having people *around* you is not necessarily having people *with* you. You can have company and still be lonely because loneliness is not the absence of another presence. Loneliness is the absence of a *suitable* presence, and everyone who is around you may not be suitable for you.

You must understand the culture and norms of that day. If you were a leper, then you were relegated to living in what was called a leper colony. You had to live with others who had the same condition as you. It was said that these colonies were made up of large numbers of persons because leprosy was a common malady of that day. You could not live in the city or come to the city. In segregation, you would live with hundreds of others who had what you had. When you read the text, however, you will notice that the Bible talks about only four lepers.

Now, in the Bible, there is never a waste of words. Many lepers lived in a colony, but only four are mentioned in the text. These four had made the decision that they refused to be counted out. That suggests to me that maybe they were the only four in the colony who refused to resign themselves to a life of "less than." Maybe they were the only four who refused to allow their condition to get into their consciousness to the extent that they felt they were what their condition said they were. No one else was with them in this dialogue, so just maybe no one else shared their attitude about their condition. These four men had the same condition, the same attitude, and the same spirit. They weren't the only ones with the condition, but they were the only ones trying to get over it! They were the only ones who wouldn't allow society to count them out. They refused to allow their condition to set the stage for how they viewed themselves in the context of the greater society. They had hope!

This text tells us, black men, to make sure we have people around who have the right mentality. Everybody who is around you may not be with you, which means that you need to get them away from you! Don't hang out with people who try to bring you into agreement with being what your situation says you "ought to be." You need to commune with people who have the right attitude. Some folk want you to stay like you are because they are living complacently in a similar situation. Misery does, indeed, love company!

Can I take it a step further? These four men were encouragement for each other, even though they all had the same issue. Their encouragement did not come from folk who weren't going through what they were going through. Sometimes you don't need a word from people who have not walked where you are walking, or who are not walking now where you are walking. Sometimes you need to be encouraged by somebody who is going through what you are going through. Non-alcoholics are not in Alcoholics Anonymous! In support groups, everyone has the same issue, but the members are there because they have the right attitude about getting out of it and over it. When my spirit gets low, I don't need somebody who isn't going through a similar situation to tell me to "be of good cheer." Instead, I need somebody to tell me that we can wait on God—together!

Your initiative will initiate God's action. Let's be theological for a minute. One of the things we always need to remember is that God is always active, even when he seems to be absent. God is always up to something on your behalf. You don't have to see God to know that he is up to something, because your expectancy and faith are not based on what you see, but on what you know! Now, here is the problem: I can't always see what God is up to, and he is not obligated to show it to me nor to give me a hint or sign to relieve me! I just have to trust that something is going on for my benefit; and when it's time for me to see that which God has in store for me, God will reveal it to me. That's a struggle. This text suggests that God makes moves where you need it. Just as important, your initiative will initiate his action in your issue.

Read the text. When you read verse 5, you discover that the lepers took the initiative at twilight. They did not just talk about it, but they did something about it! They initiated their deliverance at twilight. When you go down to verse 7, you discover that God acted in the issue at twilight. At the very same moment that they were making their move, God was making his move! There was an obstacle in their way, but God did not wait to move the obstacle when they got to the obstacle. Rather, God moved when they moved!

The minute you make up your mind and then get up and move, God will begin to move things out of your way. When you get to where God wants you to be, things will already be in place. Just like the lepers, you won't be able to figure out how it happened. But your job is not to figure it out; you job is to just enjoy it and praise God for it. If he had left it for you to deal with, you may have never gotten it. God honors your faithful initiative by moving the obstacle when you move for the opportunity. Now, the lepers would not know that God had moved it until they got to where they were going. God didn't tell them he was going to move it. He just did it. Some things you will never know—until you rise up.

If you make a move, God will move the obstacles. God honors faith and faith is not just thinking about it, but faith is *doing* something about it. When you make the move to get back in school, God will handle the obstacles. When you make the move to get the job, God will handle the obstacles. Somebody in here can testify that you got that job without the experience and still can't figure it out. Let me tell you how. You made the choice to go for it in faith, and when you made the choice, God got to the interview before you and fixed the heart of the interviewer on your behalf.

Brothers, do you have something that you need God to work out? Then make a move right now. Praise him right now! And God will start working in the place where you need it. (Now, let me balance this thing. I know what you are thinking: Some things have not moved. If it has not been moved, then that must mean it is part of God's plan. Maybe God wants to show you that he can bless you without moving the problem.)

Brothers, once you get a blessing, you must also be a blessing. God does not bless you and expect you to keep it to yourself. God blesses you so that he can use you to be a blessing to somebody else! Now, we already know that, but in this text, there is another twist. The lepers were enjoying the blessings God had waiting on them, and in the midst of it all, they had a moment of enlightenment. They said, "This is just not right. We need to let folk know what we have found." Now, remember, there was a famine in the land, so they had found some relief, and they knew that if they kept what they had found to themselves, judgment would follow. Give this some thought. The lepers didn't say they were going back to the leper colony to tell their fellow lepers what they had found. I could have felt that. No, they said, "Let us go to the king's house in Samaria and tell the king the good news."

Now, here is my problem. It was the king who put them out of the city. The king was their enemy. They wanted to go back and bless the very folk who put them out, who segregated them! God says, "Sometimes, I will test your maturity by blessing you— to see if you are willing to help and bless the folk who counted you out and meant you no good." Can you bless your enemies? Can you bless the folk who swore you would never make it? Can you bless the folk who tried to keep you from being blessed? You see, when you're really blessed, you don't have time to hold grudges, because you're too grateful.

What God gave the lepers was more than they could have ever imagined based on where they had come from. When you know what God has brought you from, you shouldn't have a problem blessing everybody and anybody else! All the lepers wanted was to live. All they wanted was life, but they got more than life; they got *life more abundantly*. When you know that God has given you life and given it to you more abundantly, it will make you rejoice. It will make you bless others.

When you decide to rise up, you not only get life, but you get it more abundantly! That's a byproduct of rising up. That's why the enemy does not want you to rise up. The last thing the enemy wants you to do is rise up, because the last time he tried to keep somebody down, he suffered his greatest defeat. The devil can't take it when people rise up, because it becomes a reminder of his greatest defeat. The last time somebody rose up on him, that Somebody got up with all power in his hands. Every time you rise up, black men, you remind the enemy that he has lost any chance of having power! Now, through Jesus, the first riser, you have the power to rise up and to be counted.

chapter twelve

from a fruitless life to a FRUITFUL life

Harold Hudson

And on the morrow, when they were come from Bethany, he was hungry: And seeing a fig tree afar off having leaves, he came, if haply he might find any thing thereon: and when he came to it, he found nothing but leaves; for the time of figs was not yet. And Jesus answered and said unto it, No man eat fruit of thee hereafter for ever. And his disciples heard it. (Mark 11:12-14)

in our text, we find jesus christ our lord teaching us a lesson about being fruitful. He gives us a lesson about looking like one thing, but actually being something else. In other words, our Master exposes us to the problem of *expecting one thing, but receiving something less than we expected!*

Jesus was on his way to the city of Jerusalem with his disciples from Bethany. No doubt, Jesus had not yet had breakfast and was now hungry. Verse 13 tells us that Jesus saw a fig tree from a distance, and it was full of leaves. It is my understanding that the first thing that appears on a fig tree when it blooms in the spring is the bud of the fruit, and then the leaves will soon follow. So, when Jesus saw the tree from afar having leaves, he went to the tree looking to find some figs. But the text says that when he arrived at the tree, he found a tree full of leaves—but a tree without any figs.

Now the text does say that the time of the figs had not yet arrived—but when Jesus saw the figless tree, he declared, "No one can eat of the fruit of this tree forever after." So, brothers, the question becomes, Why did Jesus destroy the fig tree? Why would Jesus lash out at a tree, simply because it did not bear any fruit? As you consider this question, remember, black men, that there is something that we should always remember about God—God is both good and severe!

Paul says in Romans 11:22, "Behold therefore the goodness and severity of God." We are to stress both the goodness and the severity of God, not just his goodness. Yes, you know that God is love. He is also pure and just! Yes, God does demonstrate care and forgiveness; he also holds his people responsible and accountable. Despite what some folk may believe or hope, God is not an indulgent father who is never severe. God is not weak and foolish in dealing with his children. Brothers, God never winks at our foolishness and he never excuses our unfruitfulness! Black men, this is because unfruitfulness and sin lead to destruction, and God is not a bad father who is going to allow the whole human race to destroy itself.

It goes almost without saying that God is good to humanity, but he punishes unfruitfulness so that others will bear fruit. Jesus has always acted either to teach people or to save and help us. And through the destruction of the fig tree, Jesus is teaching us a much-needed lesson. He is telling us that we need to be fruitful! Jesus is showing us that we should guard against profession of faith without bearing any fruit.

My brothers, one of the things we need in our churches is fruitful men. Why? When men are fruitful and productive, then the church of God will prosper and grow. Jesus was walking into Jerusalem in the morning. It was early morning before most people had gotten out of bed. Most likely, Jesus had been up praying for some time that morning. This suggests to us that men should always pray. Since our Lord is a praying person, then we should do the same. We all need to pray to start off the day.

Prayer makes things happen, and prayer keeps things from happening. Prayer keeps angels around us; prayer provides protection around us. Prayer keeps us in the will of God. Prayer keeps the devil and his imps away from us. Prayer keeps hurt, harm, and danger away from us.

Jesus prayed in the morning because he wanted to be spiritually prepared. The important lesson here is that it is good to be physically and mentally prepared, but it is even better, even more important, to be spiritually prepared! I see a lot of men working out to be physically prepared. They eat right and exercise to get in better shape. But it would be a good thing if more men would work out spiritually! Our families would be better, our children would be better, and our world would be better.

Jesus had been up early praying, and he had left Bethany before breakfast. Verse 12 tells us that *Jesus had a need*. His need was the same as the need we have every day. Jesus was hungry. He was hungry. He had a physical need, and his need painted a picture of his spiritual craving; it painted a picture of his ultimate longing. Jesus wants much fruit in the lives of Christians. Jesus desires to have more fruitful Christians. This is his hunger! This is his craving! This is his longing! This is the very purpose of our being—that we may have fruitful lives! In the Gospel of John, Jesus declared, "I am the vine, ye are the branches: He that abideth in me, and I in him, the same bringeth forth much fruit: for without me ye can do nothing.… Herein is my Father glorified, that ye bear much fruit; so shall ye be my disciples" (John 15:5,8).

So not only did Jesus have a need, but *Jesus also perceived potential!* The Bible says that Jesus saw the tree "afar off," a great distance away. The tree was so full of foliage, it was so full of leaves, that it appeared to be fully developed. Now this, of course, should have meant that there were figs on the tree. One would at least expect the tree to have fruit, even if it was not yet ripe. This was just a natural expectation. The full foliage, the fruitful appearance it was openly professing. The leafy appearance indicated fruit.

So it is with men and women who profess Jesus Christ. Their profession indicates fruit! The leafy appearance indicates healthiness; it indicates the lack of disease. Profession in Jesus indicates that the disease of sin has been taken care of. It has been sprayed and covered with his blood. It has been destroyed. No lying, no backbiting, no gossiping, no false promises, no shacking up, no over-the-limit credit cards, and no debt you can't pay. Profession in Jesus means that you pay your tithe; you have patience with your fellow human beings; you love all of God's children; you pray every day and every night. It means that you *walk* like you *talk*.

The leafy appearance of the tree stirred an expectation in Jesus. Jesus expected fruit to be present; Jesus expected his hunger to be satisfied by the fruit of the tree. Our profession stirs expectation among all who observe us, especially among those who are close to us. Picture the scene, my brothers in Christ. Picture the leafy appearance, the deceptive leafy appearance. The full foliage necessitates fruit. And keep in mind: profession requires that fruitfulness follow. If there is no fruit, then our profession is empty and worthless. Titus 1:16 says, "They profess that they know God; but in works they deny him, being abominable, and disobedient, and unto every good work reprobate."

But there is another point to be learned from the text. When Jesus looks at us, he sees the potential of what we *can* be—but he also sees what we *are*. In our text, not only did Jesus have a need and not only did Jesus see potential, but *Jesus also saw unfruitfulness*. And, Jesus condemned the tree's leafy profession without fruit. While standing there looking at the tree, Jesus saw no fruit. The tree had life. More accurately, the tree was existing but not really living. The tree had the sap to produce a rich foliage of leaves, but despite all the appearance of fruit-bearing, the tree had no fruit! What good is a tree that does not bear fruit? Its only purpose for existing was to bear fruit, but it failed to do its job!

In other words, this good-looking tree failed to fulfill or serve its purpose in three ways. First, it had **an empty profession**—and so do part-time Christians! They profess Jesus, but their profession is empty, hollow, or shallow. Their lives show incongruence—because their lives do not match their profession. They lack animation, behavior, works, purity, holiness, faith, and love. There is no distinction between them and the world.

The second lesson this text teaches us is that the tree had **an unfulfilled purpose.** So do part-time Christians! They profess Christ, but they continue in their own worldly pursuits, forgetting God's purpose entirely. Too many good-looking Christians who profess Jesus spend their time, their energy, and their money pursuing their own desires and ambitions—instead of pursuing God's will and purpose.

The third lesson the text teaches us is that the tree had **failed to produce.** It deceived the viewer about its productivity. So do part-time Christians. Jesus wants us to be *productive* for him. He wants us to be fruitful—and the fruits he expects us to produce are works of service. He doesn't want us just to look good, just to talk well, just to act good in front of others. Part-time Christians profess to produce, they claim to serve—and perhaps every now and then they do perform a little service, but their commitment is to themselves! Their commitment is to their business, their property, their society, and their desires. In fact, their commitment is to everything and to everyone—but God. Part-time Christians say that God is the Lord of their life, but they are just deceivers. They have no intention of serving the Lord, unless it's easy and convenient. They look at Jesus as being one of a crowd, along with everyone and everything else.

My black brothers, the Lord wants us—fathers, husbands, brothers, grandfathers, cousins, uncles, employers, and employees—to be producers of good fruit. *To be fruitful rather than fruitless!* Being fruitful means that we are doing our best to be of service to the Lord. When we are trying to be full-time Christians, then everything we do, everything we say is for the express purpose—the exclusive purpose—of building up the kingdom of God. And when we recognize that as our purpose as full-time Christians and as black men, we soon learn that the Christian life is the most *exciting* life. The Christian life is the most *thrilling* life, the most *rewarding* life, and the most *wonderful* life! Black men, the Christian life is the most *unusual* and the most *fruitful* life there is!

And when you try to be Christlike, you learn some secrets that the world doesn't know. Brothers, you see that the Christian's secret of faith is to believe in Jesus. The Christian's secret of security is to trust in Jesus. The Christian's secret of love is to know Jesus. The Christian's secret of wisdom is to learn about Jesus. The Christian's secret of assurance is to abide in Jesus. The Christian's secret of peace is to confide in Jesus. The Christian's secret of joy is to worship Jesus. The Christian's secret of growth is to feed on Jesus. The Christian's secret of happiness is to glorify Jesus. The Christian's secret of power is to live in Jesus. The Christian's secret of freedom is to stay in Jesus. The Christian's secret of safety is to hide in Jesus. The Christian's secret of hope is to look for Jesus. Black men in Christ, the real fruitful life begins and ends in Jesus!

chapter thirteen

a VISION, a voice, and an adventure
Robert C. Scott

In the year that King Uzziah died, I saw also the LORD sitting upon a throne, high and lifted up, and his train filled the temple. Above it stood the seraphim: each one had six wings.... And one cried unto another.... And the posts of the door moved at the voice of him that cried, and the house was filled with smoke.... Also I heard the voice of the LORD saying, Whom shall I send, and who will go for us? Then I said, Here am I; send me. (Isaiah 6:1-4,8)

in life, we face some surprises that simply lift us out of the rut of routine in which we have lived for years. Upon the blank pages of our lives, some things unfold and cause us to realize that a change needs to happen—and soon. Black men, many of us have a consistent daily routine. We get up, do our business, and go to bed.

Too many black men have come to believe that everything will just go on as it has for years, and that we and the world are going to last forever. Then, all of a sudden, as the sun is shining brightly, dark clouds of crisis gather from nowhere, and we are forced to face with startled eyes the bald, cruel facts of life.

For too many black men, those facts of life are dim, grim, and full of despair. As we look in our communities, we see that a lot of changes have taken place. Things will never be the same again. A crisis has unfolded right before our very eyes. Yet, we have not taken any steps to deal with the situation; we have not taken steps to prevent or reverse the situation.

Black men in America are in a state of crisis! As we look at the news, we see black men paraded through prisons like cattle going to an auction. We take note of how many black men are caught up in the drug trade, buying and selling dope. Our unemployment or under-employment rate is usually higher than other ethnic groups. Even when employed, we earn only 47 percent of the dollar white males earn. Unlike any other group, we are committing crimes in terrible proportions and being incarcerated in record numbers. Right now, there are more black men in the prison system than in all the predominately white and historically black colleges and universities combined. Although black males make up about 7 percent of the general population, they comprise more than 50 percent of the prison population. Given these statistics, not surprisingly, there is a shortage of eligible men for black women to marry. The reality is grimmer than we realize. This situation has a direct impact on the black family—as black men deteriorate, so do black families.

But that is not the end of the tragedy. The black man is far more likely to be a victim of murder. In fact he is seven times more susceptible to being killed by another black man. The black male's life expectancy is much lower than the white male's. The white woman is expected to live about 78 years; the white man is expected to live about 75.6 years; the black woman is expected to live about 71.5 years; but the black male is expected to live only 68.9 years. The black male in America is in a state of crisis, and this crisis has reached epidemic proportions!

But, brothers, crises may be lived as burdens—or transformed into blessings! We can consider the glass half empty or half full. Crises can keep us locked in dungeons of defeat—or be changed into opportunities. When misfortunes take us into the valleys of despair or cause us to lose our footing on the icy pavement of life, we often can't see God's divine plan. But every sorrow can be used to show forth God's glory if it leads us to think beyond the narrow confines of our own self-interest.

The prophet Isaiah had gone through a crisis. A king named Uzziah had died. The prophet, as a young lad, had grown up under this king's leadership. In his mind, the days of Uzziah's reign were the "good old days." During Uzziah's reign, Isaiah had no troubles to worry about. Isaiah did not have a care in the world. The young prophet, with a youth's naïve and simplistic outlook, had taken everything for granted. But, Isaiah remembered that the decisive moment of his life came in the year King Uzziah died. When the proud, successful king had been brought low by disease and passed under the shadow of death, Isaiah was called to see the eternal King.

Many of you will agree that life is full of changes. Neither rank nor worldly success can resist the attack of old age and death. How important, then, for the young man to learn that there is an unchanging Kingdom, and a King supreme in majesty and righteousness! *"Death will do it."* Death brought a change that Isaiah had to confront. This particular death was a turning point in Isaiah's existence. One day, in the same year the king died, Isaiah was in the temple. While there, he saw a vision, heard a voice, and agreed to go on an adventure. His actions provide us some insight on what we, as black men, need to do to change our lives, to change our community, and in turn, to change our world.

Like Isaiah, the first thing black men need to do is *get the right spiritual vision* to see the image of God. There are two types of vision: external and internal. External vision allows us to observe physical surroundings. Sadly, if we look at our surroundings with the physical eye, we will view some terrible things. We will behold brothers hanging on the corner, drinking forties and smoking crack. We will view black men making babies, but not taking care of them. We will see grown men in their 30s, 40s, and 50s, acting like boys in their teens. We will spot black men disrespecting our Nubian sisters and mothers. We will see the difficulties of trying to survive in a racist and economically oppressive society. With the physical eye, the black man will surely come to the conclusion that there is either no hope for him or little hope—not if we concede to a Euro-Western way of thinking. This way of thinking says "white is right."

We know that there are not enough available black men for our black women. It is getting to the point where, if a black woman wants a mate who is not on his way to jail or raising hell, she will have to look at white men. That may have to happen if black men don't step up! However, given this dilemma, why it is that when a black brother makes it in society, he has to go and get a white female to validate his worth? I don't have a problem with miscegenation. But, I can't understand why our actors, entertainers, athletes, businessmen, and politicians have to turn to white women when there are so many good sisters looking for men. Michael Jackson, I don't understand. Sidney Poitier, I don't understand. O. J. Simpson, I don't understand. Justice Clarence Thomas, I really don't understand!

And some of us won't go all the way to white women, but we are "color struck." Colorism, like racism, is alive and well. If she ain't light skinned, long haired, and tall, some of us don't even want to look. That type of Euro-Western idolatry—a sign of self-hatred—is causing us to miss our blessings and is allowing our communities to further deteriorate.

However, when we use our spiritual or internal sight, we will discover even more disturbing news. As black men, we have been tricked, fooled, and deceived into thinking that we are nothing, have nothing, and will be nothing. We have been taught that our potential is limited because we are black men. This thinking has lead many of our black men into a state of nihilism or sheer hope-lessness. Our potential has been measured or calculated by how much money we make or the material possessions we have. And there are many sisters who perpetuate this notion. There's nothing wrong with having nice things, but when material possessions control you, trouble is right around the corner! When we use our internal sight, we will discover that we have sold our souls for the almighty dollar. This has caused quite a few brothers to start selling drugs, because of the profit margin and instant gratification. They do not care if they are killing other black men, women, and children, as long as they get the money to sustain their pleasures. Pleasure is the antithesis or opposite of pain! Unfortunately, too many black men use crack or alcohol in a futile effort to escape the pain of their reality.

But (the divine conjunction but) in the bleakness of this reality, there is hope—if we can keep looking until we see the vision of God! Isaiah did not realize his potential until the year King Uzziah died, and then he saw God for himself. Isaiah was in the temple, and he saw a vision of God and God's train filled the temple. Isaiah did not realize his potential until he had come into contact with God, until God became real to him! This vision was so clear and strong that it changed Isaiah's conviction to withstand the storms and stresses of life. It came forth to shine light on the soul of this potential prophet. It gave him the power to face the people and the right to speak with rulers!

Also, this vision allowed Isaiah to look at himself and others around him differently. When Isaiah had his encounter in the temple, all he could say was, "Woe is me! for I am undone: because I am a man of unclean lips, and I dwell in the midst of a people of unclean lips: for mine eyes have see the King, the LORD of hosts" (Isaiah 6:5). In other words, Isaiah realized his own sins and the sins of others. Sin prevents us from being all God wants us to be. It deters us from our God-ordained destiny!

One of the problems with black men in America is that we have used the sins of racism, colorism, and classism as excuses to justify the wrong we do against ourselves, our women, our children, and our community. I know it's the truth. What we need is to gain some spiritual vision to correct our blurred or distorted external vision. Help me, Holy Ghost!

The next thing we as black men need to do is *hear the voice of God*. This means that we need to listen, not only with our ears but also with our hearts! Communication is critical in relationships. A human being communicates with his or her voice and body. In this vision, Isaiah noticed two types of communication from God—body language and voice. Isaiah saw God sitting on the throne, high and exalted. The body language of God demonstrated the sovereignty, righteousness, and power of the Almighty. This regal exhibition of power that was beyond human comprehension compelled Isaiah to confess his sins.

When the holy God confronts us, personal sinfulness suddenly weighs heavily on our minds. The prophet saw that we are sinners, individually and collectively; we are sinners as individuals and as communities. As I survey the congregation, I see a shortage of brothers present. Those who are not here do not hear the voice of God! If they did, they would realize that God's house is where they belong, giving thanks to God while getting power from God. However, some black men are afraid to be in the house of God and to listen to God. Why? Because God may be calling them to do some things they are not accustomed to doing.

Isaiah saw God's body language, and then he heard God's voice and was confronted with the call: "Whom shall I send? Who will go for us?" The voice of God calls us from blindness into the light. It calls us out of the abyss of hopelessness onto the trail of confidence. It calls us out of the canyon of calamity onto the road of restoration!

Isaiah saw the vision and heard the voice, and he decided to answer the call by going on an adventure with God. Brothers, when we go on an adventure with God, we are still going to have ups and down. It will not all be a bed of roses! The journey will not always be easy. Like Isaiah, you will have to confront some things. But the time has come to stand up and move in the power of God! We, as black men, need to find our strength—not in material possessions, not in our sexual prowess, not in our financial portfolio, not in our political affiliations, but rather in our spiritual life and in our relationship with God. We need to put our hope in God, our trust in Jesus, and our confidence in the Holy Spirit. We, as black men, need to abide under the shadow of the Almighty. We do not need to rely on false stimulants or trust in cunning devices. We, as black men, need to have a sense of God's companionship and helpfulness so that we will not be dependent on popularity, prominence, prestige, or power.

Today, God is still asking, "Who will go for me? Who will go on a divine adventure?" We need black men who will go for God. Brothers in Christ, we need men like . . .

- Enoch, who didn't mind walking with God;
- Abraham, who moved when the Lord said move;
- Joseph, who couldn't be persuaded by women with evil intentions;
- Moses, who told old Pharaoh to let God's people go;
- Joshua, who declared, "As for me and my house, we will serve the Lord";
- Samuel, who was dedicated to the Lord;
- Isaiah, who stood in the gap;
- Jeremiah, who didn't mind crying sometimes;
- Ezekiel, who preached to dead, dry bones;
- Daniel, who didn't mind praying;
- Amos, who told it like it is;
- John the Baptist, who cried, "Repent for the kingdom of heaven is at hand";
- Peter, who was changed from a cussing sailor to a pillar of the church;
- Stephen, who didn't mind dying for the Lord;

- Paul, who was transformed from a church fighter to a church builder;
- Booker T. Washington, who was practical yet intelligent;
- W. E. B. Du Bois, who was intelligent, yet practical;
- Marcus Garvey, who died standing up for his people;
- Adam Clayton Powell Jr., who was political, yet spiritual;
- Malcolm X, who stood up for the downtrodden;
- Martin Luther King Jr., who wasn't afraid to dream in the midst of hell;
- Samuel D. Proctor, who was erudite, yet reachable;
- Gardner C. Taylor, who is sermonic and poetic;
- Wyatt T. Walker, who is a renaissance man; and
- Nelson Mandela, who persevered with hope in the midst of it all.

Black man, have you positioned yourself to hear the voice of God? Have you designed your life so that you can see the vision? Are you ready to go on your divine adventure? My brothers, are your bags packed? God beseeches us to get on board. My black brothers, get on board! Do you have your ticket to board the Ship of Zion? Will you be ready when Jesus asks for your ticket?

chapter fourteen

home for GOOD!

Gordon A. Humphrey Jr.

Then Jesus said, "There was a man who had two sons. The younger of them said to his father, 'Father, give me the share of the property that will belong to me.' So he divided his property between them. A few days later the younger son gathered all he had and traveled to a distant country, and there he squandered his property in dissolute living. When he had spent everything, a severe famine took place throughout that country, and he began to be in need.... 'I will get up and go to my father, and I will say to him, "Father, I have sinned against heaven and before you; I am no longer worthy to be called your son; treat me like one of your hired hands."' So he set off and went to his father. But while he was still far off, his father saw him and was filled with compassion; he ran and put his arms around him and kissed him. (Luke 15:11-14,18-20, NRSV)

i pastor in a section of west oakland, california, called "Ghost Town." But it is not called that by accident. Believe me when I tell you that Oakland is a place where you can "get ghosted" real quick! At the time of this message, I am not in touch with the actual statistics, but it is sufficient to say that the murder rate reaches into the triple digits every year—which is very high for a city of proportionate size. We have a bad reputation due to the high rate of crime, violence, and drugs associated with the city. Bottom line: Oakland receives a bad rap. Consequently, the economy suffers, primarily because corporations are reticent about doing business in Oakland.

Nowhere is this dynamic more real than in relationship to our black men. Being a black man living not only in West Oakland, but also in America at large, carries with it a negative connotation. The system and the media have successfully labeled us as over-sexed, irresponsible thieves, thugs, and crooks. But I would contend that this it is not who we are by nature, even though in too many instances this is our behavior, our modus operandi.

A close look will reveal that the very people whom the government and the media have labeled as thieves and thugs are actually leaders. And, brothers, you need to know this. If there is anything I want you to glean from this message, it is that you are not what you have been called. You are a born leader! You may not act like it. Your behavior may not depict or reflect it. But the fact is that you are a leader, my brother! The reason I know that you are a leader is because you have influence—and that is what leadership is. And you have influence because you can convince your friends to do what you want, even if it's wrong!

To illustrate, you have street soldiers who will commit crimes and kill on your command. Now, say what you want to say about it, but that is leadership. It is misdirected leadership, but it is leadership nonetheless! That is the tragedy about your condition, black man. Everybody knows you are a leader. The government knows that you are a leader. White people know that you are a leader. The devil knows that you are a leader. And God knows that you are a leader. The only person running around not knowing that you are a leader is you! That is why the government and the church are helpless to do anything about the crime and violence that afflict the community, because we are trying to address the issue without input and help from you, the leaders.

The fact is that the powers that be cannot build enough prisons to stop the crime and violence in our community. And we don't have enough police to adequately address the problem. Because once we arrest one generation of criminals, another generation is waiting in the wings to take their place. Brothers, the implications are clear—instead of arresting and incarcerating the leaders, invest in them and they will put a stop to anything that you need!

I know this from personal experience. When God assigned me to my community, I made a point to walk the streets and meet the leaders. I made a point to build relationships with all of the thugs and gangsters I could. I knew that I could not influence my community without the endorsement of these leaders, because if you really want to have an influence in your community, the leaders have to say you are OK. For example, people don't break into the church, even though we are in a crime-filled area, because the leaders protect the church and they have declared the church "off limits." In a time when many pastors have security teams, I don't need one, because I have built-in security! People such as Big Tony, Crypt, Yellow, Big C, Boss Man, Smooth, and Limo, to name a few, have declared me as their pastor and Olivet as their church!

This point is worth illustrating further. As you may know, in recent years, the California prison system has used Oakland as their dumping ground for people who get out of prison. When these folks get out of prison, they are given two hundred dollars and a bus ticket to Oakland. Consequently, most of the convicts who are released are likely to return to prison in a day to a few months. A local Bay Area newspaper recently ran an article regarding the efforts of Oakland to keep parolees from going back to prison. One of the ex-convicts featured was a person by the name of Dennis Collins, his street name being DC.

Dennis is fifty years old, and he has spent thirty-four years of his life in jail. He was paroled in January of 2004—and he calls me his pastor. Many people would contend that the odds are against him. Because of his past record, housing and employment will be hard to come by. And when you don't give a former convict a chance, then naturally, he is going to go back to the familiar. The newspaper entitled the article "Home for Good?"—which was posed as a question rather than a statement. In other words, can D. C., with all of his negative history, really be home for good this time?

That is an interesting question, and one reason I am always intrigued when I read the story of the prodigal son. To me, the story of the prodigal son is the epitome of the black man in America.

If the truth is going to be told—and it seldom is—the black man is not an evil and wicked creature to be detested and feared. The black man is often a lost individual who needs to be reclaimed. Black men, we are the strongest and most brilliant people on the planet, but we have lost our way, and we need to be found and then reclaimed!

Just like the prodigal son, we used to be at home in the Father's house. But because we have fallen into the trap of society and Satan, we have left home and we have lost our way. And I believe that we are lost for several reasons.

we don't know our history

First, we have lost our way because we don't know our history. History is defined as the past events in a period of time or in the life and development of a people, an institution, or place. You see, brothers, there are events in our past that have contributed to our present condition. Black men, we are in trouble and at risk of extinction! But we did not recently or haphazardly get to this point. A series of events have contributed to our lack of development. And someone has rightly stated that those who are ignorant of their history are destined to repeat it! That is why it is interesting to me that, some forty years after the civil rights movement, we have more rights and opportunities, but our condition has worsened. We are in danger of losing the rights that we fought so hard to gain!

In my community, black men will hurt you if they feel like you are disrespecting them, trying to use them, or trick them. But the government and white people have been playing tricks on you for four hundred years. They disrespect you every day of your life, but you are not angry with them! And the reason you are not angry with them is because you have not studied your history enough to understand what they have done to you and how you were systematically placed in this predicament. Therefore, if the black man is to come home for good, he must first revisit his authentic history and not somebody else's version of his-story.

we have misplaced our values

Second, we have lost our way because we have misplaced our values. In other words, things that used to be important to us are not important anymore. My father, Rev. Gordon Humphrey Sr., is a great man of God in his own right. And, recently, he shared some information with me about our family tree and his early upbringing. Interestingly enough, my dad never knew his own father. His father died when he was three years old. Consequently, his older brother, Handsome Humphrey, raised my dad. When my grandfather died, Handsome quit school so that he could go to work and take care of the family.

This was during the Depression, when people were on relief and the government used to have bread lines. And in my father's community, they would give away bread at the fire station. People would stand in lines for hours to receive this bread. So, one day my grandmother sent my dad down to the fire station to get some bread. Uncle Handsome had to pass the fire station to get home from work. On that day, he saw my dad in the bread line. He walked up to my dad and pulled him out of the bread line. Then, he went home and told my grandmother that he did not ever want to see her or any of his family standing in a bread line, as long as he had his health and strength. For men like Uncle Handsome, it was beneath their dignity to accept "handouts."

When I heard that story, it became evident to me that the black man has left the Father's house. In that, we have misplaced our values. Men used to take pride and value in making provision for their families. Now too many of us are willing to abdicate our responsibility to our children and our mothers. That is to say, it is not as important as it used to be for us to be known as "the man of the house" and providers for our families. Notice when our women speak of our men, often they won't say, "That is my husband" or "He's the father of my children." Instead, they say, "That just my baby's daddy." Therefore, if the black man is truly to return home for good, he must first regain his sense of pride, and then he must restore his godly value system as it relates to what is important.

our behaviors are unhealthy

Third, we have lost our way because our behaviors are unhealthy. The Bible says that the prodigal son wasted his substance in riotous living. And when I look at the current generation of young black men whom we are raising, I would have to say that they are the most brilliant and creative generation we have ever seen. They are also the most reckless and unrestrained generation I have ever seen!

Too many of our young men are willing to play games and take too many unnecessary risks with their lives. In Oakland, our kids have what is called "sideshow." A sideshow is where the youth get in their cars and drive recklessly and dangerously at high speeds in the streets. Brothers, haven't all of us looked at our people and wondered what has gotten into their minds—what allows them to do some of the crazy things that we see them doing?

I would contend that the reason we see so many of our people in general—and our young men in particular—taking risks and engaging in this reckless behavior is that they don't know that their lives have value! I heard Jesse Jackson say once that, in our minds, black life has become cheap. That is why we shoot and kill each other quickly and indiscriminately. That is the reason we engage in activity that we *know* will eventually take us to jail or to the cemetery—because somewhere in this journey called life, this system has sold us on the idea that our lives don't have value. And when you don't value your life, you will play games with it. But, when you come to the realization that your life *does* have value, you don't play with it, nor do you allow anybody else to play with it either! Therefore, if the black man is to be reclaimed and return home for good, he must rehabilitate his behavior and rid himself of his unhealthy lifestyles.

we have left god

Finally, we have lost our way because we have left God. The Bible says that a famine arose in the land and the prodigal "began to be in want." So, he hooked up with a landowner in the area, and the man gave him the job of feeding the pigs. But the Bible says that it didn't take long before the prodigal "came to himself." And when the light came on in his heart, it sent a message to his head, at which point he said, "I have no business living like this."

This is what I want my brothers to know. You have settled for something less than what God has designed you for, and you have no business living like this! You are unemployed and have no marketable skills that you can point to, but you have no business living like this. You are making children that you don't take care of, but you have no business living like this. You are a frequent resident in prison, but you have no business living like this.

Black men, you are the original man on the planet! You are a giant, and Satan has you acting like you are a midget. God has a better way for you to live. All he is asking and waiting on is for you to come home. God is waiting with open arms to receive his sons. God is not going to force you to return home, but it is his desire for you to return home. He would love for you to do more than just visit. He wants you to return home for good. He wants to put a ring of mercy on your finger. He wants to place a robe of grace around your body. He wants there to be celebration of Jubilee on your behalf. He has already sacrificed a calf in the form of a Lamb on your behalf.

This message is as much for the church as it is for black men because the Bible says that as the son was making his way home, when the father saw him making the effort to return, he ran out to meet him. I want the church to know that the black man is coming home! He is on his way back to the church. But, know that when he comes home, he won't be clean. He will have some mud and dirt on him because he is coming from the hog pen of life. Some of our brothers will be coming with guns and AK-47s. Some of them will be coming home with crack addictions. Some of them will be coming home with alcohol addictions. Many of them will be coming home with warped value systems. But, they are coming home!

The question is, Will the church run out to meet them—or will we stand and wait to see if they fail or fall? That is my challenge to the church, as well as the black community and family. Every time one of our men makes the effort to come home, let us run out to meet him! And when he arrives home safely, let's throw a party!

If we run to meet them, we can answer the question "Are our men home for good?" with a resounding yes! We will have made a decision that, where our men are concerned, "home for good" is not a question; only one answer is acceptable. Every time one of our men makes the effort to come back to God, we must proclaim and believe that he is "home for good"!

section four

TRUMPET SOUNDS to address
the INTRA-PERSONAL ILLS of our day
(part two)

chapter fifteen

the COURAGE to be (YOURSELF)

Jamal-Harrison Bryant

> And Saul said unto David, Go, and the LORD be with thee. And
> Saul armed David with his armour, and he put an helmet of
> brass upon his head; also he armed him with a coat of
> mail.... And David said unto Saul, I cannot go with these; for
> I have not proved them. And David put them off him. And he
> took his staff in his hand, and chose him five smooth stones
> out of the brook, and put them in a shepherd's bag which he
> had, even in a scrip; and his sling was in his hand: and he
> drew near to the Philistine. (1 Samuel 17:37b-40)

my brothers, at the time of this writing, there are
more than six billion people on this great planet we call Earth.
One of the awesome wonders of God is that, of these six billion
people, not one of them is exactly alike. Of these six billion people, not one of them has had the identical experience. However,
if we would allow Jesus in our lives, all of us have one thing in
common—the opportunity to have a personal savior!

In the Old Testament, we find a relationship with God that
blessed and cursed people simultaneously, but we were never able
to gain one accord. When Jesus came, he broke the boundaries
of what many people allow themselves to do as a part of a group
philosophy. There are so many churches that are practitioners of
illegal cloning because they want everybody to shout the same,
speak in the same tongue, wear the same hat, adorn themselves
in the same colors, and bring the same Bible. But, they are going
against the New Testament legitimacies of individuality. What

Jesus wants all of us to honor and own up to is that God made us as individuals. As individual people, he gave us a distinctive personality, as well as unique characteristics. This is your personal I.D.—your identification. Your I.D. is a function of your individual personality, and it shows that only you are you. Another man may have the same first name as you, but he is not you. Another man may share your last name, but he is not you. Another man may have both of your names, but he is not you!

In large part due to terrorism, you are required now to show your photo I.D. before boarding a plane. This I.D. must have your photo, as well as your personal information. If not, you are considered an impostor. Now, those of you who are not interested in moving anywhere or going anyplace, you don't have to show I.D., but for those of you who have your mind on straight, for those who have someplace in this world that you want to go, and for those who have visions that you want to fulfill, God wants you to show your I.D.!

"What do you mean, Preacher?" No prayers ought to be identical because everybody's needs are different. That's why you have to find your own praise, your own worship, and your own relationship with God. That's why you have to carve out your own distinctive way of praising God! No one can tell you how to praise God because no one really knows what it took for you to praise God the way that you do. Brother, you need to take a look at yourself in the mirror. You need to take ownership of what you see. You don't have to be afraid of who you are. You don't have to wonder if God made a mistake in making you. You just need to have the courage to be yourself!

Every person has a distinctive set of life circumstances that brought you here. But, the wonderful thing about God is that he can use one preacher to affect 1,300 people in 1,300 different ways. The same sermon delivered to 1,300 people will be received in a multitude of ways—because we see with not only our eyes, but also with our experiences. We hear with both our ears and our experiences! You have to see and hear from the view of your unique circumstances. You have to understand now that every time you come to church and you begin to praise God, you're showing your I.D.—because your praise is a reflection to the celestial bodies of what you are and what it is that you're going through.

That's why I cannot come to church and get in other folks' business. I don't know what they are going through. I don't know their personal I.D. So when I come to church, I'm not thinking about the folks who are behind me or in front of me. I come in church, I worship God, and act like it's just the two of us.

Brothers, we need to take a course in ontology one on one. Ontology is the metaphysical study of being. Ontology is the science of understanding one's own being. Paul Tillich, a well-known German theologian, understood this when he wrote a book that shares the title of this sermon: "The Courage to Be." In the preface of this book, Tillich says that courage can show us what being is, and being can show us what courage is.[1] What are you saying, Paul Tillich? He is saying that you have not discovered courage until you are secure in your own being. When we are secure in our being, then we have courage. In other words, you cannot intimidate me when I know who I am, and there is no way you can make me afraid of myself when I know what God is calling me to be!

The Bible tells us, "Greater is he that is in you, than he that is in the world" (1 John 4:4). When I have courage, then I understand Paul's words to Timothy: "God hath not given us a spirit of fear; but of power, and of love, and of a sound mind" (2 Timothy 1:7). Dear brothers, I hope some of you will get courage before this message is over. This means that you will no longer fear bill collectors because you know that there is nothing they can do to you—because even if you get evicted, you know that God already has another house with your name on it!

Tillich further posits that courage is the ethical act in which a human being affirms one's own being, in spite of an environment that is against one's self-affirmation. The only thing that gives me courage is when I can defy what other people tell me I'm unable to do. Brothers, I'm talking about folk who try to talk you out of your dreams, try to convince you out of your calling, try to persuade you out of your anointing. You have to believe that if God told you so, it *will* come to pass. No matter how long it takes, trust in the Lord with all your heart!

Few of us like opposition. However, we don't find our courage until we come against opposition. Some of us have never found the fortitude for our own being because we've never been opposed. One of the sweetest victories you could ever accomplish in life is succeeding in the face of people who wanted you to fail. The reason God keeps our enemies close is because he wants them near enough to see what a miracle looks like—and so you can see that miracle reflected in the face of folk who told you it could not happen. Brothers, you can do all things through Christ who strengthens you!

Brothers, what do you fear? What are your fears? What stops you from dreaming and having the courage to move forward?

The first thing that stops us from acquiring the courage to be ourselves is that *we are afraid of our past.* You'll note in our Scripture text that David heard there was a man by the name of Goliath who was talking trash about his God. David says, "I have to go fight." Now, it would have been easier for David not to go. It would have been easy for him not to go because he was just used to herding sheep, or because he was the youngest, or because other folks were more experienced or better equipped. David could have come up with a litany of excuses—but he didn't. Brothers, we must stop making excuses! Stop making excuses about why you are where you are. "I would have finished college, but I got a girl pregnant." "I would have started my business, but my momma got sick." "I would have joined the church, but I messed up too bad to become respectable now." We're afraid of our past.

The second reason some men are afraid to be ourselves is that *we are afraid of our problems*. David's obvious problem was that he was facing a giant. On top of this, no one believed he could win the battle. Thus, David also had to face the problem of his family not believing in him. Some of you are unable to be yourself because you place so much value on what your family thinks of you. Here you are, forty years old and you are still allowing your family to call you "Little Man" and "Boo Boo." Your family needs to know that you are not the boy or young man you used to be. Some of you better get ready, because the folk you have to get straight, quite often, are in your family. Some of them keep trying to block you from going to the next level!

When we devote too much concern to what others think about us, we start to question our own abilities. We begin to feel insecure and uncertain. When we put the opinions of others too close to what God has instructed us to do and to be, we begin to allow their questions to irk us. They want to know, "Why do you keep going down to that church?" They want to know, "Why do you read your Bible so much?" They want to know, "Why are you always going to prayer meetings and Bible study?" You can hear them in the next room, saying things like, "He thinks he's fooling some-body; I knew him when he used to be a mess." Brothers, stop act-ing like you don't hear them and go confront them. Brothers, walk in the power that God has given you. Have the courage to be you!

Brothers, the third reason we are afraid to be ourselves is that *we are afraid of our unknown potential*. A person's potential reflects the future, and the future is uncertain. Most of us are good at telling others how to take care of their business. It's safe to give advice to somebody else because you're looking at their life. But, when you step out on faith—with your *own* life—you're going to another place where you don't know how it's going to end. When you step out on faith, you're saying, "I believe in the power of God." That's why we should never judge our life based on what other people are experiencing—because we don't know what it is that God has in store for us!

Whatever God has just shown you to this point is only a preview of the future. God is saying, "Look, if I'm able to do it for them, then what do you think I have in mind for you?" And every now and again, you ought to thank God for the possibility! I don't know what God has in store for me, but whatever it is, it's got to be better than what I have right now. In our text, the Bible says that Saul came to David and said, "All right, you're going to fight the giant. Let me put my armor on you because this is what worked for me. I want to put my mantel on you because this is what took me through some of my storms." Brothers, let me help you. Sometimes, when you have a battle, you can't take advice from other people, because your battle is not exactly like their battle. There is some stuff going on in your storm that is unique; therefore, you must be ready to solve your problem in the way that God leads you to do so. You must have courage to listen to God's will for your life, and use the equipment he has given you to solve your problem. Brothers, you must have the courage to be you, no matter what the situation entails or who it involves.

Not long ago, I went to Atlanta. While there, I went to Morehouse for my ten-year college reunion. While I was walking through the campus, reminiscing and reflecting on all of the things that God did for me while I was a student there, I wanted to shout every time I thought about what I went through back then. I remember going through one whole semester eating Oodles of Noodles! I remember having to make grilled-cheese sandwiches with an iron! Brothers, I ain't playing with you today. I remember going to the cafeteria on somebody else's meal plan. I better not tell it all…!

Well, my trip down memory lane was interrupted when I was approached by one of the deans. My former dean said, "Jamal, let me see you for a minute." He said, "Jamal, I'm proud of you." I said, "Thank you, Dean." He said, "I'm proud of you—but I'm concerned." I said, "You're concerned about me? You have all these students here on campus. Why are you concerned about me?" He said, "Jamal, I saw your broadcast the other day." I responded, "Oh, did you? Thank you for watching. Now, tell me your concern." He said, "Jamal, I just heard that you were accepted into Oxford." I said, "Yeah, Dean, I was accepted into Oxford." He said, "I'm proud of you." I said, "Thank you." He said, "I heard you graduated from Duke with honors. I'm so proud of you." I said, "Thank you." He asked, "You're a third-generation preacher, aren't you?" I said, "Yes, I am." He responded, "I'm proud of you, but I have a concern. Didn't you go to Africa to live for a year in the Study Abroad Program?" I said, "Yes, I did." He said, "If my memory serves me correctly, you were one of my well-cultured students." I said, "Oh, Dean, thank you." He said, "Jamal, you were one of those students that, within the first two bars of music, could decipher between Mozart and Bach." I said, "Dean, that's me." He said, "You knew the difference between the pictures of Gordon Parks and James Venderneer." I said, "That's me." He said, "You knew the poetry of Maya Angelou and William Shakespeare." I said, "Yeah, Dean, that's me." He said, "With all that going on, I don't understand why you are in church screaming and sweating like that. Jamal, I just want to give you a bit of advice. If you would just lower your voice, be a little bit calmer, a little bit more collected—I'm telling you, Jamal, if you listen to me, you'll sell more tapes. Not only that, they will invite you to be in some bigger conferences." He said, "Jamal, just put on a three-piece suit, put on a plain solid tie, get rid of those gators, put on some Florsheim shoes, and you could be a respectable preacher."

I looked at him and said, "Dean, can I talk now? Can I say something for just a little while? I don't mean any disrespect, but I gotta preach to you because I finally got the courage to be myself." I said, "When I first started out, I tried to be T. D. Jakes, so I would say 'Get ready, get ready, get ready!' When I grew further along, I tried to be like Leroy Thompson and said, 'Money cometh to me right now!' I tried to be like John Hagen and said, 'Give him praise and glory!' I tried to be like Joel Oleson and said, 'Well, friends, today I want to talk about forgiveness.' I tried to be Frank Reid and said, 'Somebody, say Yeah!' I tried to be Walter Thomas and whistle a few times. I tried to be Rod Parsley and said, 'America needs a revival.' Dean, I tried to be like all of them, but none of that fits me! You have to understand that I ain't nothing but a ghetto preacher. I may not have a three-piece suit, I may not have the most expensive shoes, but now, I do have the courage to just simply be me." Therefore, I'm just a little black boy from west Baltimore who can say, "Preach, black man."

Brothers, you must have the courage to be yourself! There comes a time when you have to shout the way the Lord is leading you. You have to rejoice like the Spirit is guiding you. You have to praise him in your own way. Brothers, when all is said and done, in the end, you must have the courage to be. Brothers, we each have our own personal, God-given I.D. Have the courage to be yourself!

NOTE

1. *Paul Tillich.* The Courage to Be. *(New Haven: Yale University Press, 1952), preface.*

chapter sixteen

when GOD hooks a BROTHER up

Frederick D. Haynes III

And unto Joseph were born two sons before the years of famine came, which Asenath the daughter of Potipherah priest of On bare unto him. And Joseph called the name of the firstborn Manasseh: For God, said he, hath made me forget all my toil, and all my father's house. And the name of the second called he Ephraim: For God hath caused me to be fruitful in the land of my affliction. (Genesis 41:50-52)

it is impossible to feel good in a relationship with someone else when you feel bad about yourself. We cannot have a healthy relationship externally when there is something within us that is sick internally. Why? Permit me to offer an illustration.

I believe it was the year 1973 and my favorite boxer, Muhammad Ali, was in a match with Ken Norton Sr. I was blown away while I watched, because for some reason my hero, Muhammad Ali, was not fighting his style of fight. In round twelve, the announcers had already surmised that, unless Ali rallied to close with a ferocious finish, he was, in all probability, going to lose the fight. I was a fan of Ali. Ken Norton had been having his way with the greatest boxer of all time. Muhammad Ali, who could "float like a butterfly and sting like a bee," in this fight had lost his wings and has lost his sting. Round twelve and Ali wasn't fighting like I was accustomed to seeing him fight. By round twelve, he was simply holding his guards up and fighting from a defensive position only. He wasn't finishing the fight with a fury of punches. Ali lost the fight to Ken Norton Sr. And I was hurt and devastated. I later learned that Ali had sustained a broken jaw in round two. Ali wasn't able to fight his fight in the later rounds because he had suffered a broken jaw in an early round of the fight. In that early round, Ali experienced brokenness, and as a consequence, for the rest of the fight he was fighting out of character. Although those watching could not see or detect his brokenness, he was broken.

Let me go ahead and exegete existentially the experience of Ali. All of us can relate to the experience of some brokenness in the early rounds of life. Now, remember that unless you were Ali, you did not know about the broken jaw. Why? Because we cannot tell by looking at a person what brokenness he or she has experienced. We cannot judge people by how they are on the outside. As a matter of fact, a lot of people who have sustained some internal brokenness and/or damage will try to compensate with some external cosmetic adjustments. In a real sense, some of us will do everything on the outside to camouflage and cosmeticize what is really going on in the inside. Brothers, we need to admit that many of us have been damaged in the early rounds of our lives. Some of us are broken because of our father's departure in an early round of life. Some of us are broken because of a tragedy experienced early in childhood. And this brokenness has often convinced us that we need to live our lives in a defensive position.

Do you know anybody who spends all of life in a defensive posture? Do you know people who are spending their lives trying to avoid some stuff they think is going to happen to them? They're always in a state of defense. I know there's somebody, right now, living life in this dangerous disposition. You feel much better, you feel at "peace" when you're in a defensive mode—when you're biting at someone, when you're playing against someone. You view people as adversaries and not as allies because in the early rounds of your life you found yourself subjected to some suffering and some pain. Perhaps you've tried to trust before, but eventually you promised yourself that you would never trust anyone again.

Many people can relate to this, but I'm sure black men in particular feel a connection. Why? Because whenever we find ourselves having been hit hard with a punch of despair, pain, or grief in the early rounds of life, we immediately put up our defenses and we move through life in a posture of defense. There are some brothers who just play hard. They take the position that they will never allow anyone to hurt them again. They want to be seen as tough and rough, so nobody will get over on them. They've got to play hard because they're not about to get punked. You know, there are some black men moving through life, and their thing is "I'm going to play hard. I'm not going to get played like a violin again in my life. I'm not going to let somebody get close to me or get next to me. I'm not going to trust anybody anymore, and I'm just going to play hard."

Not only are there brothers who play hard, but also there are brothers who say, "I'm going be a control freak. I am going to control any situation or any relationship I am a part of. I'm going to control what my woman wears. I'm going to control what time my woman calls me. I'm going to control what my woman does on her job. I'm just going to control the level of involvement my woman has with her family and friends." And controlling brothers will oftentimes play enough mind games with a sister to make sure he keeps her under his control. He'll threaten to walk out on her. He'll threaten to hurt himself. He'll threaten to do all kinds of crazy stuff just to emotionally manipulate a sister and keep her under his control. There are brothers who will either play hard so they won't get punked or they will control situations and people in an attempt to avoid being in a position of vulnerability.

Finally, there are brothers who don't play hard, who don't try to control, but whose thing is "Hey, I'm not going to let anybody get close enough to me to hurt me. I'm not going to open up and share with you from my heart. I'm not going to let you know what I'm really feeling or thinking. I'm going to simply shut down. I'm not going to open up. Why? Because I've spent some time in heartbreak hotel during the early rounds of my life and I'm not going to experience that pain again."

Brothers, I know that I'm talking to you. I know that I'm all in your business. In the early rounds, you've been hurt and you've spent the rest of your life in a disposition of defense. You're playing hard, you're a control freak, you're not letting people get close to you, or you've made up your mind that you are going to just settle for being a maintenance man. "I'm not going to have a real relationship. I'm going to have as many honeys as I can have and not make a commitment. I'll just be their maintenance man. I'll give them pipe when they need their plumbing fixed. I'll be the maintenance man, because I'm not going to open up my heart and experience a real relationship, because I don't want to get hurt anymore in my life." Unfortunately, too many of our brothers have never seen a healthy relationship. They've never seen a man truly love a woman in a holistic fashion, so they find it difficult to be in a healthy relationship. This is one of the reasons so many counselors recommend long-term therapy for our African American brothers.

Notice if you will from Genesis 41:50–52 that if anybody was a candidate for some long-term therapy, it was Joseph. Joseph was a candidate for some serious, long-term therapy. After all, every relationship Joseph had up until he was thirty had left him in pain and "to'up from the flo'up." Check out the relationships of Joseph's early life. It begins before chapter 37 of Genesis where Joseph testifies that he grew up in a household that was fraught with baby mama drama because of his daddy's other women. You remember that Jacob had another wife named Leah as well as some concubines on the side. Joseph's daddy was hurting and breaking the heart of Joseph's mother, Rachel. As a consequence,

Joseph's mama, Rachel, was heartbroken, and any young boy who really loves his mama doesn't want to see his mama's heart broken. It was messing with Joseph. And then, watch this, while Joseph is still a teenager, his mother dies. The apple of his eye, the one he loves so much is dead, and Joseph is still a teenager. There's baby mama drama and on top of that, his mama has died. Joseph is a candidate for some long-term therapy.

Then after that, his own family rejects him. His brothers hate him for something that he doesn't have anything to do with. You see it is one thing for folk you don't know to reject you; it's another thing when folk who share your blood, your DNA, and your biological background reject you. That can sabotage your self-esteem. That can mess with your mind. That can break your heart. That can cause you to require some long-term therapy.

Joseph was also sold into slavery and had to deal with the enduring legacy, aftermath, and residuals of repressive slavery. You do understand that slavery objectives and signifies people? As black men, we've got to deal with the residual effects of slavery, because it still has a lingering effect on African American men. Do you know that in slavery, black men were reduced to baby-making machines? That meant that men were not supposed to commit to a woman. The worth of a man was determined by how many children he had and by the number of women he could have them with. You think that's just back in slavery? Well we've got some men in 2004 who may not have shackles on their feet, but they have chains on their brain, because it does not take a man to make a baby. It takes a man to raise that child. I don't care if you're not with that woman anymore. If you got that woman pregnant, the least you can do is help that woman, respect that woman, and help raise your child.

Not only was Joseph enslaved, but to make matters worse, a woman had the nerve to step on him and lie on him. Joseph is a candidate for some long-term therapy. Sister Potiphar comes to

Joseph, but when she comes at him, Joseph says, "I can't go out like that." She then lies on him. Joseph is then not believed by Potiphar, the man he had worked so hard for. Potiphar threw Joseph in jail for something he did not do. I tell you, Joseph was a candidate for some long-term therapy.

While in jail, Joseph helps out the butler. Joseph says, "When you get to the palace, don't act like Clarence Thomas and Condoleeza Rice and forget where you came from, but make sure you turn around and reach back and help a brother out." The butler gets to the big house and forgets about Joseph. Now I'm trying to tell you, Joseph was a candidate for some long-term therapy. Look at all the trash, trauma, dysfunction, and drama that characterizes the background of Joseph's life. But hold on before you give up. The book says that Joseph stepped up and became the Prime Minister of Agriculture. God turned the tables completely around on his situation. A slave became a number one stunner. A prisoner became Prime Minister. The one who was in the prison is now chillin' in the palace. Joseph is now a big baller and shot caller because God is the only one I know who can bring those who are on the bottom up to the top.

Brothers, if you are in a bad situation right now, don't you know that God specializes in stepping into bad situations? But wait, Joseph's healing isn't complete until God hooks him up. God hooks Joseph up with an African honey named Asenath. Joseph married an African honey, an Egyptian sister. You know she was fine. I'm talking about Beyonce, Halle, and Ashanti all combined. I'm talking about fine. I'm talking about the girl can wear some Apple Bottom jeans and make all the heads turn. I'm talking about an African honey. The Bible says that Joseph married Asenath, the daughter of Potipherah, who was a priest in Heliopolis. Understand that in Egyptian culture, priests were often the best educated. Asenath grew up in a household of a well-educated father. Understand that in the Egyptian culture, women were not held down as less than men, but women were seen as equals. Many of the great Pharaohs and leaders in Egypt were sisters. It was sisters like Nefretiria who gave leadership.

So, as a consequence, Joseph married into a culture with a woman who had been raised in the principles of *Maat*. *Maat* is the Egyptian value system of balance that means life should be approached not in an imbalanced fashion of all head and no heart, where it's all body but no spirit. No, there is a balance to life especially in the context of a relationship. Joseph was able to experience his healing, because God hooked him up with what he needed. When God hooks a brother up, he is hooked up indeed. Asenath helped Joseph realize that love at its best is holistic.

Brothers, if you want to experience the ultimate in intimacy, you must understand that love is not just physical. Physical is what you see. Understand that a whole lot of folk may look good to you, but they're not good for you. Brothers, you have to look beyond a sister's external appearance, you have to look at her internal qualities as well. You want to see the character behind her clothes. You want to look beyond her face and see if she possesses some faith. You want to look beyond her weave and see if she got some wisdom. You want to look beyond where she lives and see how she's living. So the *Maat* concept of balance applied in the relationship.

God hooked Joseph up with an African honey who was able to help him in three ways. How do you know when God has hooked you up with a true woman of God? *Whenever a woman helps you gain a new perspective, whereby you can trace God's hand in your hell and in your hurt, you've been hooked up by God.* Look at this Egyptian sister, she's saying, "Baby, I know the early rounds of your life have left you with some haunting memories that really hurt, but God was by your side all along. Listen, I know things aren't going like you want right now, but you know I'm praying for you and I have your back. Baby, you need to understand that

God is preparing you to do something great in your life. You may not see it right now, but God is getting you ready for a better tomorrow. I know you're feeling down right now, I know you feel broken right now, but God is not through with you!"

Watch the text. When Joseph and Asenath have their babies, guess what he names them? He names the first child Manasseh, meaning forget, because "God made me forget all the hell I went through," and the second child Ephraim, which means fruitful, because "God made me fruitful in the land." Joseph didn't just say he was forgetting because he didn't care anymore. He didn't just choose fruitful because he was good. He said, "God made me forget and God made me fruitful." You see, when you've got the right woman in your life, she's going to put God in the sentence of your life. Once God is the subject of your sentence, you become the direct object of your subject. See, when God is the subject, you begin to say, "Hey, I've been through hell, but that's okay because I now know that the Lord was with me." If God is your subject, you say, "God of our weary years, God of our silent tears, thou who has brought us thus far along the way!" Asenath said, "Listen, Joseph, you know why you are where you are? Because God hooked a brother up. All you've been through, God's been ordering your steps. Protecting you from dangers, seen and unseen." Brothers, we just can't thank God for stuff that we can see; we also have to thank God for things that we have not a single clue have been done on our behalf. There's a whole lot of stuff you did not see that did not happen because of God's hand in ordering your steps.

Brothers, I got something else—a sister will not only help you gain a new perspective, *a sister will show you how to assume a pardoning posture: a pardoning posture whereby you get over whomever and whatever tried to take you under.* Let me tell you something. When folk do you wrong, don't you ever just think about getting back at them? I'm only talking to people who've had their hearts broken. I'm not talking to those whose everything has been fine in their lives. All of us have had our hearts broken by somebody. When it first happened, didn't you at least just want to do something one time to those who broke it? Brothers, don't do it; that's holding a grudge. That's becoming embittered. That's allowing what they've done to you to get inside of you. And whenever you are resentful and you hold a grudge and can't stand someone because they have dissed you, and dogged you, broke your heart, it's just like you're drinking poison and hoping they get sick from it. You drink the poison, but instead you hope they get sick because you drank the poison. It doesn't work like that. Whenever you do that, you're simply giving them energy that they don't deserve. Most of them folk ain't thinking about you anymore. They've moved on with their lives. You're still mad. You're still tripping. Don't you give them that kind of victory. Let 'em go on about their stuff and just know that God will handle God's business.

I was in Omaha preaching, and a brother came up to me after church. He said, "Man, I loved your sermon. You told my story. You just blessed me." His wife was there and he said, "She'll tell you. I was one bitter black man. I could not even receive the love of this wonderful woman right here because of the stuff that went down in my household. My father abused me and my mother. I used to helplessly watch my mother get beaten by my father. As a consequence, I really didn't have a concept of how to relate to a woman other than what I saw at home. Do you know I nearly acted out what I'd seen at home with this wonderful woman God gave me? One day I came home mad and I slammed stuff around. She said, 'Baby, what's wrong?' I raised my fist and she said, 'Listen now, you may want to think about what you're doing because I am the cousin of the sister who poured grits on Al Green, so you do not want to mess with me right now.' So, I came to my senses. We went to counseling and the counselor kept telling me, 'Man, you've got to let this go.' I said, 'but I can't let it go. I can't let go of what my father did to me. I can't let go of my mama allowing it to happen.' And then, Pastor Haynes, we went on vacation. On vacation, we were on a ferry going to an island. The ferry sprang a leak. When the ferry sprang a leak, it began to sink. When it began to sink, a rescue helicopter began to rescue those of us on the ferry. I had brought two bags of souvenirs I collected. Well, my wife climbed up the ladder. I came to the ladder with both bags in my arms. I reached for the ladder, but of course I couldn't go up the ladder because I had too much baggage in my arms. The rescue worker looked down at me and said, 'You've got to leave those bags alone. Let those bags go if you want to be saved.' When he said that it dawned on me, he ain't just talking about my souvenir bags, but God was talking about my other baggage. He says if you want to be saved, you gotta let them go. Then my wife says, 'Come on, baby, I need you. Let the bags go. If you want to be saved, you've got to let it go.'" You know that you have been hooked by God, when your woman encourages you to let go of baggage from the early rounds of your life and assists you in seeing your self-worth and your value to her, to your community, and to your God.

And finally, brothers, *a good sister can show highlights of how God can exercise God's power and will from some unlikely places.* God'll give you the power to blow up in the same place where you were torn down. Brothers, keep in mind that God made Joseph fruitful in the land of his suffering. God doesn't always have to take you out of your situation to bless you. God can bless you in the midst of the most horrible, hellified situation you ever found yourself in. God doesn't have to take you off your job to bless you at your job. God can keep you on your job and bless you in front of all your haters. God doesn't have to give you a new spouse to bless you. Brothers, God can bless you with the beautiful and dynamic woman that you have right now. God can hook you up with the sister who is in your life right now. Brothers, God can show you what it means to love in an authentic, holistic way. Holistic in that you are loved mind, heart, spirit and body.

When the two of you fall in love by way of each other's mind, you know you have more than a "love jones" because the minds are motivated. Your thoughts are stimulated and activated. You're always striving to move beyond where you are to the next level. You know that you've got somebody when you talk and will not let each other settle for settling with what you've been thinking. Love on the mental level can bring something out of you that you never thought that you could think about.

Then there's love on the emotional level. Emotional simply means that you feel some things that you didn't know you could feel. Feelings that go deep, deep, deep down inside. So much so that you sing with Luther Vandross about the "Power of Love," or with Baby Face about "Whip Appeal." You see "whip appeal" is a byproduct of love. There aren't any words to describe what's going on with the two of you. And as a consequence, you begin to communicate on a heart level, which is more than what you can think about. As you communicate from the heart, you know your heart will be protected. You won't get judged, you won't get talked about, and you won't get criticized. You'll just be affirmed because you're sharing from your heart.

Mind, heart, and then there is spirit. When you connect with someone on a spiritual level, that means your connection with them is divine. Because your connection with them is divine, you can pray together. That means you can study God's Word together, which brings you closer to God together. Your relationship resembles the spokes of a bicycle wheel that connect at a hub. God is the hub. The closer the two of you get to God, the closer you get to one another. You've got a "jacked-up" relationship if you aren't any closer to God because of the one you're hooked up with, but you've got a "Jesus-up" relationship when the closer you get to Jesus, the closer you get to one another.

When that balance is there, in comes the physical. When two are hooked up spiritually, it impacts, influences, and energizes your sexuality and your sensuality. Brothers, it's time out for talking about sex in the club, sex in the barbershop, sex in the beauty shop. Now, you need to come to the church and get hooked up under the authority of God's Word and discover what sex is supposed to be like. You haven't had any sex until Jesus gets in it. You haven't had any sex until the Holy Ghost fills you up. And when both of you are filled with God's spirit, that's when it's on!

Brothers, you haven't been hooked up until God hooks you up. You haven't experienced true intimacy until you've experienced divine intimacy. You haven't experienced true love until you've experienced love that has been ordained by God. Brothers, if you want to get hooked up by God, you have to be hooked *with* God.

chapter seventeen

thank god for GOOD MEN!

Jeremiah A. Wright Jr.

> Now there was a man in Jerusalem whose name was Simeon; this man was righteous and devout, looking forward to the consolation of Israel, and the Holy Spirit rested on him. (Luke 2:25, NRSV)

after preaching the sermon "ordinary men" at our church, I gave an altar call for the men at that worship service who wanted prayer, who wanted to rededicate their lives to Christ and who wanted to do it God's way, to come forward to the altar.

The men not only came forward to surround the altar; they encircled the pulpit and the chancel area in our sanctuary! There were five hundred men standing for Christ around the pulpit. It was a sight to behold. Envision it: Black men standing for Christ. Black men, brave men, "bad" brothers standing for Christ. Somebody said to me, "When have you seen that many black men standing together? And it wasn't for football. It was for the Father!"

It was not for basketball; it was for the balm in Gilead. It was not to drink whiskey; it was to get drunk with the Spirit of God. Five hundred black men in one building, not to protest the government, but to proclaim God's gospel and to praise their God. Imagine it—five hundred black men standing together, not because they were incarcerated, but because they were liberated. Not because the law had locked them up, but because the Lord had set them free!

My brothers in Christ, when a man has been with Jesus, it makes him bold. It gives him courage. Then it gives him conviction, and ultimately, it gives him a case of the "can't-help-its."

You can't help but tell somebody how the Lord has raised you up and how the Lord has picked you up, and how the Lord has done something for you that you could not do for yourself.

"What can wash away my sins?" The legality of Islam? No! The meditation of Buddhism? No! The dietary laws of Adventism? No! The high holy days of Judaism? No! The philosophical constructs of Emmanuel Kant? No! The intellectual vacuum of atheism? No! The epistemology of deism? No! The theology of James Cone? No! The sociology of Max Weber? No! The psychology of Asa Hilliard? No! The strange sound of hieroglyphics? No! The familiar tones of gospel music? No! "What can wash away my sin? Nothing but the blood of Jesus!"

When the Lord has done something for you that you could not do for yourself, you can't keep the good news to yourself. When you accept him for yourself, you can't hold back on his praises. When the Lord empowers you to climb the steepest mountains, you can't lift your hands high enough. When the Lord takes you through some stormy situations, you can't thank him enough. When the Lord makes a way out of what appears to no way, you get a terminal case of the "can't-help-its."

You can't help but tell somebody what the Lord has done for you! You can't help but speak in his name. You can't help but lift him up. You can't help but stand on his promises. You get courage, you get conviction, and you get a permanent case of the "can't-help-its."

It is sad to say, brothers, but we always hear so much about the "bad" men. The irresponsible men. The men who make babies, but who don't take care of babies. The men who are caught up in the prison system. The men who are lost to the gangs or deep into drugs. We always hear about the men whom the sisters can't find. In fact, how many times have you heard sisters say "All black men are…" Next time you hear them say that, tell them, "No, the Bible says there are some 'good men.'"

We always hear about the bad men. If we don't see them on Oprah, we see them on Sally Jesse Raphael. If we don't see them on Geraldo, we see them on Montel. If we don't see them on Gail's show, then they are on Jerry Springer's show "duking"!

We always hear about the bad men, but this text says that there are some good men. *Thank God for good men!* Luke gives us a picture of two good men. In Luke 2:22, it was one month after the "first Christmas" when the time came for the purification of Joseph and Mary. One month after Jesus had been born. That is when the purification ritual took place, according to the Law of Moses.

In this passage you find Joseph, a good man, bringing Jesus, along with Mary, up to Jerusalem to present him to the Lord. Joseph is bringing Jesus to church. Joseph is bringing his son to the church. Joseph didn't send Mary by herself. He didn't tell Mary, "Well, you go on, take the boy." He didn't tell Mary, "I don't have to go to church to worship God; I can worship him at home." This is a good man bringing his wife and child to church. Imagine this—you have Joseph bringing the child to church. You have Joseph doing what the Law of Moses says you are supposed to do for a child. You have Joseph taking care of and providing for Jesus. Joseph, who was crazy in love with Mary, this text says, is a good man who is taking care of a child! Good men take care of their babies—even when it *ain't* their baby. That is a good man!

Now, in five short verses about another good man, Luke gives us seven characteristics of such a man.

Characteristic 1: *A good man is a man who is righteous.* There was a man in Jerusalem whose name was Simeon. This man was righteous. Being righteous does not mean you are perfect. It means you are in a right relationship with God. A good man talks to God because he is in a right relationship with God. He also listens when God talks back to him. "The steps of a good man are ordered by the LORD" (Psalm 37:23, KJV).

A good man is a man who is *righteous*. Simeon, the Bible says, was righteous. He was in a right relationship with God. He talked to God, and he listened when God talked to him. He went to church. He studied the Word of God. He was looking forward to the consolation of Israel—to the one who would save and comfort God's people. A good man is a man who, like Simeon, is righteous. This is a precept found in the Word of God.

Characteristic 2: *A good man is not only righteous; he is devout.* That means that he has a devotional life. "Devout" means he attends to the life of the Spirit. He is engaged in some spiritual exercises, and he is just as faithful with them as the brothers who are running to the gym three and four times a week are faithful to their physical exercise regimen.

Brothers, a good man has some spiritual exercises. To put it another way, he bends his knees in prayer. He lifts his arms in praise. He raises his hand in supplication. He presses the pages of the Bible to swell his heart—not bench presses to get "swollen," but he presses toward the mark for the high calling of the prize, which is in Christ Jesus. He presses for salvation. He runs, not a quarter of a mile in under one minute. He runs, not five miles every morning, but he runs this race with patience, and he runs and does not get weary. He walks, not just around the track at a football field. He walks, not just around somebody's park, but he walks by faith and not by sight. He walks and does not faint. He has some spiritual exercises. He has a daily devotional life that does not depend on somebody making him do it. A good man is devout.

Characteristic 3: *A good man trusts the promises of God.* Simeon was looking forward to the consolation of Israel. Why? Because that consolation was promised by God. A good man trusts the promises of God. How can you tell if he trusts God's promises? Well, see if he takes God at his word. How does he do that? Does he worship God as God tells him to worship? God makes certain promises concerning worship: "Where two or three are gathered in my name, I am there among them" (Matthew 18:20). Does the man take God at his word and gather in the presence of other men and women of faith? Does he pray as God tells him to pray? "If my people who are called by my name humble themselves, [and] pray, ... then will I hear" (2 Chronicles 7:14). That is another promise. Does the brother take God at his promises?

Does he tithe? If you hear a man say, "I ain't giving my money to any preacher," you don't have to ask any more questions. He has already told you that he does not take God at his word—that he doesn't trust the promises of God. Because it was God who said—not the preacher—God said, "Bring the full tithe into the storehouse, so that there may be food in my house, and thus put me to the test, says the LORD of hosts; see if I will not open the windows of heaven for you and pour down for you an overflowing blessing." Here comes the promise: "... see if I will not open the windows of heaven for you and pour down for you an overflowing blessing" (Malachi 3:10). Brothers, do you trust the promises of God? Jesus said—not Jeremiah Wright—but Jesus said, "Give, and it will be given to you. A good measure, pressed down, shaken together, running over, will be put into your lap; for the measure you give will be the measure you get back" (Luke 6:38). A good man trusts the promises of God—in tithing, in prayer, in worship, and in all facets of life and faith.

Characteristic 4: *A good man has a relationship with the Holy Spirit.* In Luke 2:25, it says of Simeon: "The Holy Spirit rested on him." Have you ever been around somebody on whom the Holy Spirit rested? I don't mean they've got long faces and long dresses and are unattractive. That is not the Holy Ghost; instead, that is some cultural norm. The presence of the Holy Spirit brings a peace, and it brings a power that is awesome and magnetic. You just enjoy being in that Spirit-filled person's presence. In verse 26, it says, "It had been revealed to him by the Holy Spirit ..." The Holy Spirit talks to a good man.

In his prayer life, the man must stay still long enough to let God speak to him and reveal to him what it is the Holy Spirit wants. Verse 26 says: "It had been revealed to him by the Holy Spirit that he would not see death before he had seen the Lord's Messiah." The Holy Spirit rested on him. The Holy Spirit talked to him. The Holy Spirit directed him. Brothers, you must let the Lord lead you because the Lord will never lead you astray. A good man such as Simeon is guided by the Holy Spirit.

Characteristic 5: *A good man is a man who knows who Jesus is.* Simeon was not confused about the Lord's identity, even as an infant. He knew who Jesus was. He didn't think Jesus was one prophet among a long list of many other prophets. He knew who Jesus was. He didn't wonder whether there was some other path to salvation, and he didn't argue about whether he just might be mixed in with some other ancient African tradition. Simeon was a good man, and *he knew who Jesus was.*

A good man knows Jesus is Lord. He knows Jesus is a rock in a weary land and shelter in a time of storm. He knows Jesus is the only begotten son of God the Father. He knows Jesus is Mary's baby. He knows that Jesus is a tear drier, a strong tower, strength for today and bright hope for tomorrow. He knows that Jesus is the source of his strength and the joy of his life. A good man knows Jesus is worthy of all of the praise. A good man knows that Jesus is, without a doubt, the Lamb of God and the Savior of the world. A good man knows who Jesus is.

Characteristic 6: *A good man is a man who embraces Jesus.* Then the Scripture says Simeon "took him [Jesus] in his arms" (v. 28). That means a good man is not ashamed to embrace Jesus. When you embrace Jesus, that means you can say, "He's *my* Savior. He's *my* rock. He's *my* salvation. He's *my* joy. He's *my* hope. I don't care what some other religion says about him. I embrace him! You can't make me doubt him. I know too much about him."

A good man is a man who embraces Jesus. He embraces Jesus as Alpha and Omega, the beginning and the end. He embraces Jesus as his bread when he's hungry and his water when he's thirsty. A good man embraces Jesus as the fairest of ten thousand, and as the bright and morning star. He embraces the truth that Jesus is Joshua's battle-ax, Ezekiel's wheel in the middle of a wheel, and Jeremiah's fire shut up in his bones. A good man embraces Jesus as Lord over his life. He embraces Jesus as the author and finisher of his faith. He embraces Jesus as a way out of no way, a bridge over troubled waters, a mother for the motherless, and a father for the fatherless. He embraces Jesus as a friend to the friendless. A good man knows that Jesus is a burden bearer and a heavy-load sharer. The text shows us that Simeon embraced Jesus. We as black men must also embrace Jesus, if we desire to be good men.

Characteristic 7: *A good man is not ashamed to praise God.* Luke 2:28 says, Simeon "took him in his arms and praised God." Simeon praised God. What I like about this passage is that Simeon's praise is not caused by somebody outside of his person. When he embraced Jesus, he started praising God. His praise didn't come about because somebody coerced it. His praise didn't start because somebody in the temple said, "You ought to praise him." His praise did not originate because the temple praise team was up trying to pump up the crowd. His praise flowed out of a heart that had been in the presence of the Lord. A good man, when he has been in the presence of Jesus, will praise God. And praise is spontaneous! Praise is authentic. It is open. It is honest. Praise is joyful.

This text doesn't say a thing about what Simeon did for a living. It doesn't say a thing about what kind of car he was driving. Lexus isn't in the text. Benz is not in the text. It doesn't say that he made six figures. He might even have had some dirt up underneath his fingernails. What the Bible says is that Simeon, a *good* man, was righteous; he was devout; he trusted in God's promises and had a relationship with the Holy Spirit; he knew and embraced Jesus; and he wasn't ashamed to praise God.

Brothers, don't miss being a good man by looking at the wrong list! Look at this list in Luke's Gospel. Throw your list away! Get a new list—and let God transform you into the good man he can use for his glory.

chapter eighteen

what makes YOU so GREAT, black man?

Darryl D. Sims

And they compel one Simon a Cyrenian, who passed by, coming out of the country, the father of Alexander and Rufus, to bear his cross. And they bring him unto the place Golgotha, which is, being interpreted, The place of a skull. And they gave him to drink wine mingled with myrrh: but he received it not. (Mark 15:21-23)

in times such as these, so many of us—too many of us—have damaged self-images. We turn on the TV and see images of black men that are stereotypical, degrading, debilitating, and humiliating! We read the newspaper and digest so much about black men that is negative. We turn on the radio and cannot escape hearing African American men being bashed. Seldom is our greatness as a people discussed in honest and accurate dialogue by others. Seldom is our greatness discussed—even among ourselves!

In times such as these, we all need to be reminded of a simple but powerful theological truth, which is *God does not make junk!* I don't know about you, my brothers in Christ, but when I look in the mirror, I don't see junk. Instead, I see greatness, because I am made in the image of God. My lips, my hair, my skin tone, my nose, and my body are creations of greatness. How do I know this to be so? Because God knew me in my mother's womb and it was he who formed me (Psalm 139:13-16)—and God does not make junk!

In times such as these, black men must be able to find a glimmer of bright hope in the midst of dark times. In times such as these, we need to be able to have some assurance amid so much chaos and self-doubt. In times such as these, our people, our men need to champion the promises of God the Father, God the Son, and God the Holy Ghost, like never before. Brothers, you know the promises that I'm talking about, don't you? I'm talking about the promise that says, "I will never leave thee, nor forsake thee" (Hebrews 13:5). I'm talking about the promise that says, "He only is my rock and my salvation" (Psalm 62:6). I'm talking about the promise that says, "God is our refuge and strength, a very present help in trouble" (Psalm 46:1). I'm talking about the promise that says, "No weapon that is formed against thee shall prosper" (Isaiah 54:17). Brothers, I'm talking about the promise that says, "Come unto me, all ye that labour and are heavy laden, and I will give you rest. Take my yoke upon you, and learn of me; for I am meek and lowly in heart: and ye shall find rest unto your souls. For my yoke is easy, and my burden is light" (Matthew 11:28-30).

In times such as these, our nation needs to be reminded of who is really in charge of this thing called life and this place called Earth. The nation needs to be reminded of a text that says, "If my people, which are called by my name, shall humble themselves, and pray, and seek my face, and turn from their wicked ways; then will I hear from heaven, and will forgive their sin, and will heal their land" (2 Chronicles 7:14). This nation needs to hear from us, black men, "that at the name of Jesus every knee should bow, of things in heaven, and things in earth, and things under the earth; And that every tongue should confess that Jesus Christ is Lord, to the glory of God the Father" (Philippians 2:10-11).

In times such as these, we need to recapture the love that once existed in the church. We, as fathers, husbands, brothers, uncles, grandfathers, and sons must get back to one fundamental principle of life, which is "Charity starts at home." We must get back to loving our neighbors—even when our neighbors don't love us. Black men, we must return to loving one another as we love ourselves and as Christ loves us. To do this, we must allow Jesus to be Lord over our every decision. Why? Because these are the things that made our people, our black men included, so great!

The wayward lifestyles that we are living hinder our effectiveness at disciplining and witnessing to our family. Why do you smoke when you know what this does to your body and lifespan? How can you tell your children to attend Sunday school if you don't attend classes yourself? How can you expect your soul mate to respect the pastor if you speak negatively about the servant of God? How can you tell your children to respect their elders when you don't even speak to your mama or daddy? Black men, what on God's green earth makes you feel that sisters should cater to your every need when you refuse just to say those three little words that she needs to hear—you know these words—"I love you"? How do you expect her to warm you up in the midnight hour when you are so cold to her during the day? My brothers, how will our black family members know what true love is if we don't display it to them? Think about it—how will the little black boy know how to love a black girl if he never sees his black father (or any black male) love his black mother properly? How will that young lady know the difference between a male's love and a male's lust for her, if her mother has nothing positive to say about any male? How will our children reach their full potential in life if we, the adults, don't make them a priority? Brothers, how will our families know of their greatness if you talk only about their weaknesses? Ultimately, the question becomes, How will our children and soul mates stand like kings and queens if we talk to them and treat them like they are thugs, riff raff, or second-class people?

Let's look at the question in a different way: How does a black man who does not know of his own greatness tell and show his loved ones their greatness? Although there are so many questions to be answered, there is really only one answer: Teach them the ways of Jesus the Christ. The Bible says, "Train up a child in the way he should go: and when he is old, he will not depart from it" (Proverbs 22:6).

The more I read the Bible, the more convinced I am that respect—as fathers, sons, brothers, husbands, and soul mates— must be earned by living as a dignified, Christian man. The Bible says, "Ye are a chosen generation, a royal priesthood, an holy nation, a peculiar people; that ye should shew forth the praises of him who hath called you out of darkness into his marvellous light" (1 Peter 2:9). Anthropologists have proven that humankind originated in Africa. And as the Bible says, God made the first human being from the black dirt, not from the white snow. Paul said, in the book of Philippians, that he was a Hebrew of Hebrews (Philippians 3:5); translation: I'm blacker than midnight! What does this mean? It means that we, like Paul, need to be proud of our heritage. It means that being black is a part of my greatness. It means that God knew what he was doing when he made me.

My African American brothers, do you want to know how to be the greatest that you can be? Do you want to know what makes you so great, black man? Do you want to see the relationship between God and your greatness? If you are really ready to walk in the greatness of what the Lord expects of you and has to offer you, then let's see what this biblical text suggests. The text reveals at least three things that make you so great!

your legacy in christ

First, black man, you are so great because of your legacy in Christ. Abraham paid tithes to King Melchizedek, an African king of Salem and a priest of the Most High God. This African brother is one of the most controversial people in the Bible. Who was the man? Some scholars argue that he was the pre-incarnate Christ.

Some scholars argue that he was the patriarch of Shem. Some scholars raise the argument that he was simply a Canaanite priest-king who worshiped the Most High God. Whatever the case may be, *this* preacher is arguing that Melchizedek is a part of our rich and stolen legacy in Christ. It is essential for us as black men to see the connection between this African king and our Christ!

Look at how the writer of the book of Hebrews lays out the connection between this African man and Christ. The writer points out that Melchizedek was "without father, without mother, without descent, having neither beginning of days, nor end of life; but made like unto the Son of God; abideth a priest continually" (Hebrews 7:3). Verse 4 goes on to say, "Consider how great this man was, unto whom even the patriarch Abraham gave a tenth of the spoils." This was a great black man! This seventh chapter in Hebrews clearly compares the ministry of Melchizedek, King of Salem (or King of Peace), with the ministry of our Lord Jesus the Christ. Why should this matter to us as black men? It shows that our legacy as a people of color is directly connected to Jesus!

Furthermore, I say without reservation or hesitation that the One whose blood can wash away our sins traveled through the lines of Africans! Our legacy in Christ runs deep within the antiquity of the Bible because the Bible says that Moses was a Hebrew. The Hebrew people are black. It is believed that Moses was raised under the black pharaoh, Seti I. However, when Moses killed an Egyptian, whom we know was black, he fled to the land of Midian. My brothers, Midian is in Africa!

And there is more … Cyrene is modern-day Libya, which is also in Africa. This is good news for those of us who are of African descent. John L. Johnson says in the *Black Biblical Heritage*,

> Phut was Ham's third son; the scriptures do not mention any of his sons by name, but it is certain that he had sons from whom the Lybians or Cyrenians are descended. These people were located on the upper northern part of Africa

and their principal city was Cyrene. They played a vital role during and after the crucifixion.[1]

I share this information to make a simple point: God always used the African soil and the African people as conduits to bring about his will and desires for the entire human race. We, as black men, must learn of our rich legacy, and we must see how our rich legacy is directly attached to Christ.

your labor for christ

Second, black man, you are so great because of your labor for Christ. Being able to play basketball or football is good. Being a doctor or lawyer is good. However, only that which you do for Christ shall last. As a people who profess to be disciples of Christ, we must always remember whom we represent. Our labor must be tied to the will of God and to the betterment of all people.

During the Civil War, Harriett Tubman was an agent for the North—and she helped hundreds of slaves to get freedom. She was a modern-day Moses. Benjamin Banneker was an ingenious scientist who lived during the Revolutionary War era. He created an almanac[2] that white and black farmers would use for years to come, and his predictions of the weather were more accurate than that of the leading white scholars and of Benjamin Franklin's *Poor Richard's Almanac*. More recently, Dr. Charles Richard Drew became a pathology instructor at Howard University Medical School. As a surgeon, Dr. Drew was fascinated by the problem of preserving blood for surgical transfusions. He had seen many surgery patients go into shock and die due to blood loss because hospitals could not easily preserve fresh, ready-to-use blood. Why not? Blood tended to spoil quickly by coagulating, or thickening and forming clots—small masses of blood cells clumped together. So, Dr. Drew started investigating this problem. While experimenting with plasma, the part of the blood that remains liquid outside the body, he discovered that it had the same effect as whole blood when used in transfusions. More importantly, plasma could be stored for a long time under refrigeration, whereas whole blood lasted only a week. Plasma also had the advantage of working for everyone whereas whole blood had to match each patient's unique blood type.

As the lives of Dr. Charles Drew, Harriet Tubman, Benjamin Banneker, and untold numbers of other African Americans suggest, our people have always carried the load of other people. And as men of God, we must be willing to continue that legacy—for Christ's sake. When we allow our labor to be Christ-driven, racism will not be the prevailing thought on your mind. When you seek to do God's will, hatred toward you can't deter you. When you seek to do God's will, glass ceilings can't suppress your dreams. When you seek to do God's will, failure will serve as fuel and your stumbling blocks will be your stepping stones.

Struggles are not unique to blacks, because every group has to bear a unique cross. We all have a cross to bear! Simon was compelled to carry the physical cross for our Master, and we as men of divine color must continue in the spirit of Simon, this black man from Cyrene, and carry the cross of Jesus today. Simon loved Jesus enough to carry the cross, and Jesus loved Simon enough to carry his sins away! We are bought with a price because although Simon had to bear a wooden cross for Jesus, Jesus had to carry the sins of the world on his shoulders. "He was wounded for our transgressions, he was bruised for our iniquities: the chastisement of our peace was upon him; and with his stripes we are healed" (Isaiah 53:5). Why? Because "God so loved the world that he gave his only begotten Son" (John 3:16).

your life belongs to christ

Third, black man, you are so great because your life belongs to Christ. Although our forebears had to bear the brunt of slavery, sharecropping, Jim Crow, segregation, discrimination, isolation, and alienation, they remained *faithful* to God. In the midst of their pain, our forebears remained faithful. And now, we, the children of great people, must also believe that he is the author and finisher of our faith. God shows us that he will bless our faithfulness. God will bless a person's faithfulness by blessing their offspring.

In Romans 16:13, Paul sent salutations to Rufus, an eminent individual in the community of faith. This was the same Rufus who, as a youth, witnessed his father being kicked into the ground and compelled to carry Jesus' cross. Simon had passed down his faith to his son. Now, Rufus could have given up on serving Christ when he saw the injustices of the people in power. But he knew that, somewhere along the line, trouble wouldn't last always. Somewhere along the line, he knew, a change had to come. Somewhere along the line, he knew, weeping may endure for a night, but joy will come in the morning light. Somewhere along the line, he had been taught that "the LORD is my shepherd; I shall not want" (Psalm 23:1). Somewhere along the line, he had been told that "the LORD is my light and my salvation; whom shall I fear?" (Psalm 27:1). Somebody had taught that little black boy about the sayings of the prophet: "He giveth power to the faint; and to them that have no might, he increaseth strength; even the youths shall faint and be weary, and the young men shall utterly fall; But they that wait upon the LORD shall renew their strength; they shall mount up with wings as eagles; they shall run, and not be weary; and they shall walk, and not faint" (Isaiah 40:29-31).

Black men, this is why we sing the song "Great Is Thy Faithfulness":

Great is thy faithfulness, O God my Father;
There is no shadow of turning with thee;
Thou changest not thy compassions, they fail not;
As thou hast been thou forever wilt be.

Great is thy faithfulness! Great is thy faithfulness!
Morning by morning, new mercies I see.
All I have needed, thy hand hath provided.
Great is thy faithfulness, Lord, unto me![3]

Black men, you are great. Black men, God does not make junk. Black men, God does not make mistakes. Black men, God does not create people for the expressed purpose of destroying them. Black men, God loves you. God will be faithful to your efforts, to your families, to your hopes, to your pains, to your fears and to his promises. And so, black men, God needs you to stand up—because God needs you to be great ... for him.

NOTES

1. *John L. Johnson.* Black Biblical Heritage.

2. Benjamin Banneker's Pennsylvania, Delaware, Maryland and Virginia Almanack and Ephemeris for the Year of Our Lord, 1792; Being Bissextile, or Leap-Year, and the Sixteenth Year of American Independence *(Baltimore, Md.: Goddard & Angell, printers),* 1797.

3. *"Great Is Thy Faithfulness." Words by Thomas O. Chisholm, 1923.*

about the contributors

Charles G. Adams has since 1969 served as pastor of Hartford Memorial Baptist Church in Detroit. Prior to that, he was pastor of the historic Concord Baptist Church in Boston. His extensive writings include a sermon that appeared in Judson Press's *9.11.01: African American Leaders Respond to an American Tragedy.*

Jamal-Harrison Bryant is pastor of the Empowerment Temple in Baltimore, Maryland. He received his M.Div. degree from Duke University.

Frederick D. "Freddie" Haynes III has since 1983 served as senior pastor of Friendship-West Baptist Church in Dallas, Texas. The church, known for its efforts in faith-based community development, has in the last decade grown from about 500 members to over 8,000.

Jim Holley has for more than three decades served as pastor of the historic Little Rock Baptist Church in Detroit. He was recognized by the *Detroit Free Press* as one of the top five ministers in Michigan.

Harold A. Hudson is pastor of Calvary Tremont Missionary Baptist Church in Columbus, Ohio. He is a past moderator of The Eastern Union Missionary Baptist Association and a member of National Baptist Association U.S.A., The Ohio Baptist General Convention.

Gordon A. Humphey Jr. is pastor and chief visionary at Olivet Institutional Baptist Church in Oakland, California. His "Sunday Night Live" service, which welcomes people to come as they are to experience God without judgment or condemnation, has been modeled across the nation.

Tyrone P. Jones IV is the fifth pastor of the historic Messiah Baptist Church in Bridgeport, Connecticut. He is a 1998 graduate of Howard School of Divinity in Washington, DC, where he was awarded the W.O. Carrington Award for "Most Gifted Preacher."

Claybon Lea Jr. is the pastor of Mt. Calvary Baptist Church, Fairfield, California. He received his B.A from Morehouse College, M.Div. from Union Theological Seminary in New York, and his D.Min. from United Theological Seminary in Dayton, Ohio.

Rodney Maiden is senior pastor of the Providence Baptist Church in Cleveland, Ohio. He is the president of The Edifying Word Ministry and has a weekly broadcast called "Edifying Word."

R. W. McKissick Jr. is senior pastor of Bethel Baptist Institutional Church in Jacksonville, Florida. He holds an M.Div. from the Samuel DeWitt Proctor School of Religion at Virginia Union University and a D.Min. degree from United Theological Seminary in Dayton, Ohio.

Joe S. Ratliff has since 1980 served as pastor of Brentwood Baptist Church in Houston, Texas. Named "Minister of the Year" in 1985 by the National Conference of Christians and Jews, Dr. Ratliff is co-author of the Judson Press book *Church Planting in the African American Community.*

Robert C. Scott is pastor of Central Baptist Church in St. Louis, Missouri.

J. Alfred Smith Sr. is senior pastor of the Allen Temple Baptist Church in Oakland, California. The author of sixteen books, he also serves as Professor of Christian Ministry and Preaching at the American Baptist Seminary of the West in Berkeley, California.

Frank A. Thomas is the senior pastor of Mississippi Boulevard Christian Church in Memphis, Tennessee, and serves as the Co-Executive Editor of *The African American Pulpit*.

Lance D. Watson is senior pastor and chief visionary of the Saint Paul's Baptist Church in Richmond, Virginia. He is host of the national telecast "Positive Power" and author of the books *Maximize Your Edge: Navigating Life's Challenges* and *That Was Then, This Is Now*.

Jeremiah A. Wright Jr. is senior pastor of Trinity United Church of Christ in Chicago and the author or editor of several Judson Press books, including *What Makes You So Strong?*, *Good News!*, and *From One Brother to Another II*.

Johnny Ray Youngblood is senior pastor at the 8,000-member St. Paul Community Baptist Church in Brooklyn, New York. He is also the author of the best-selling book *Upon This Rock*.